A 40 DAY ADVENTURE, GETTING CRAZY ABOUT JESUS

DR. DAVID L. CLARK

"I AM" Crazy
Copyright © 2016 by Dr. David L. Clark
All rights reserved.
Printed in the United States of America
ISBN: 1536871753
ISBN-13: 978-1536871753

Cover design by Scott Fulk
Interior design by Scott Fulk
Edited by Daryl Saladar and Robin Benskin

DEDICATION

In loving tribute to Jesus, the great "I AM," whose mercy is unending. Enthralled with His redemptive grace, I will be "I AM" crazy forever.

To Central Christian, who has kindly allowed me to serve as pastor for the best 35 years of my life.

To my Deby, nothing in my life or ministry would be possible without her.

CONTENTS

HOW TO USE THIS BOOK 1
DAY 1 3
DAY 2 9
DAY 3 15
DAY 4 21
DAY 5 27
DAY 6 33
DAY 7 39
DAY 8 45
DAY 9 51
DAY 10 57
DAY 11 63
DAY 12 69
DAY 13 75
DAY 14 81
DAY 15 87
DAY 16 93
DAY 17 99
DAY 18 105
DAY 19 111
DAY 20 117
DAY 21 123
DAY 22 129
DAY 23 135
DAY 24 141
DAY 25 147
DAY 26 153
DAY 27 159
DAY 28 165
DAY 29 171
DAY 30 177
DAY 31 183
DAY 32 189
DAY 33 195
DAY 34 201
DAY 35 207
DAY 36 213
DAY 37 219
DAY 38 225
DAY 39 231
DAY 40 237

A 40 DAY ADVENTURE, GETTING CRAZY ABOUT JESUS

HOW TO USE THIS BOOK

This book is not intended to help you speed-date with Jesus. A real relationship is only crafted over the process of time. This book is designed for a personal encounter with Jesus daily for forty days.

Set aside all your concerns for several minutes each day. Better yet, *"Cast all your cares on Him, for He cares for you"* (I Peter 5:7 NIV). Once you have yourself right, take a deep breath, and settle into the Lord's presence. Open the book and just do the reading for that particular day. Jesus wants to show Himself to you. Take some time to get a sense of who He says He is and how He wants you to know Him. Spend the rest of the day pondering what you read and hopefully what you experienced with Him. Do that for forty days, and my prayer is that you will go "I AM" crazy (in a very good way).

This book is also not intended to provide stand-alone spiritual nourishment. Your soul needs a balanced diet. Daily time, interacting with Jesus, is essential. But you must add to it meaningful time with His people. So to wring every drop of benefit from this journey with Jesus, in addition your daily reading, make two commitments: 1) engage in "I AM" Crazy worship at church each weekend for praise and preaching; and 2) join one of our "Crazy" small groups to do the adventure with others who are growing in Jesus.

By the way, at the end of each day's reading, you will find a way to practice what you've read. There will be a Crazy Big Idea. Try to commit these to memory. Just think, in six weeks you'll have forty big ideas on who Jesus is; your relationship with Him; and what He is excited to do in your life when you're excited enough to let Him.

There's also a Crazy Scripture to memorize each day. You can do this. Write it on a piece of paper. Stick it in your purse or your pocket. Carry it with you throughout the day. Ask God to bring it to your mind. You can pull it out and read it repeatedly. Write it on another piece of paper and stick it on your fridge or bathroom mirror. Do what it takes to make these scriptures a part of who you are. In just 40 days, you will have the mind of Christ, the great "I AM," to help you flourish in His likeness.

Finally, after you read each day, engage Jesus personally with a Crazy Prayer Starter. These are not to be all you pray. These "starters" are meant to ignite a fire of prayer in your soul. You talk to God and burn with desire for Him to talk back. It's a relationship.

I can't wait to see you in 40 days. I can't wait for you to see me. Let's get "I AM" Crazy!

This whole book is all about Jesus and how we can be "I AM" crazy. Today is day one of our "I AM" crazy experience. Today our spiritual adventure begins, as we launch a 40-day journey with Jesus! Forty days to become "I AM" crazy—crazy about Jesus!

It seems like everyone has their own idea about who Jesus is. From Fox News to the New York Times to our next door neighbor, everyone has their own opinion on Jesus: savior, good teacher, crafty charlatan. Who's right? Who's wrong? Does it matter?

What if Jesus chose to introduce and explain Himself? How might He do it? We don't have to guess because Jesus did just that. And it does matter because He did it numerous times, all in the writings of John.

Over the next forty days, we will step into thirteen distinct moments with Jesus as He reveals who He is to us and what He does for us with His famous "I AM" declarations, like: "I AM the Light of the World!", "I AM the Bread of Life!", "I AM the Good Shepherd!", "I AM the Door!", "I AM the Resurrection and the Life!"

Maybe you say, "Big deal. So Jesus used metaphors to describe Himself. What of it?"

Personally, I am more disturbed by the metaphors Jesus used for refusing to surrender to who He is and what He longs to do for us. In a word, it is hell. Jesus described this place of everlasting torment (Luke 16:23) as "darkness" (i.e., Matthew 8:12; 22:13; 25:30). Hell will be pitch black, solitary confinement forever. A second metaphor Jesus used for hell was "gnashing of teeth" (i.e., Matthew 8:12; 13:42; 22:13). At that time, this was an idiom, indicating regret. Hell is an eternal experience of agonizing, emotional anguish. Finally, Jesus described hell as a place where the "fire" does not burn out (i.e., Matthew 13:42; 25:41; Mark 9:43; Luke 16:24). This is what existence looks like without Jesus.

Just as He goes to great and dramatic lengths to warn us away from the pain of not surrendering to Him as Lord, so Jesus compels us with these different "I AM" expressions to experience the pleasurable joy of knowing Him truly and fully (John 15:11).

Over the next forty days, Jesus will reveal to you personally what He wants to do for you; how He wants to heal and help you. He will show you how He can be your comforter and your counselor. He will make plain how He can lead and guide you along a path where everything works together for your good. The bottom line is Jesus wants you to know He is able to strengthen and sustain you—to strengthen and sustain your relationships, to strengthen and sustain you physically, financially, mentally, and emotionally. And what Jesus says He will do for you, He can do for you because Jesus is God.

DAY 1

If this is the first time you have heard or read the declaration that Jesus is God, you might think, "This is messing with my head. If God is God, how can Jesus be God, too?"

That is the all-important question. In fact, how you live out the answer to that question determines your eternal destiny—heaven or hell. A bunch of murderously angry, really religious Jews killed Jesus based on how He answered that question. Every single time Jesus made one of His famous "I AM" statements, it was His way of claiming to be as much God as God the Father is God.

The most prolific writer in the New Testament, the Apostle Paul, absolutely believed Jesus to be God. This grabs my full attention because, for the longest time, Paul did not believe Jesus to be God. He wanted Jesus dead. He hated all who believed in Jesus and wanted them dead. But in a personal, life-changing encounter, our Lord introduced Himself to Paul this way: *"I AM Jesus, whom you are persecuting!"* (Acts 9:6 NIV).

So check out then what Paul wrote of his belief in Jesus to the church in Philippi: *"Jesus Christ...had equal status with God!"* (Philippians 2:6 MSG).

Here's what Paul wrote to the church in Colossae: *"We look at this Son and see the God who cannot be seen!"* (Colossians 1:15 MSG).

Writing to all Jewish people, Paul penned these words: *"The Son is the radiance of God's glory and the exact representation of His being, sustaining all things by His powerful Word!"* (Hebrews 1:3 NIV).

John, Jesus' very best friend, opens his book on Jesus with these staggering words: *"In the beginning was THE Word*

(Jesus), and THE Word was with God, and THE Word was God. He was with God in the beginning!" (John 1:1,2 NIV).

I capitalized "THE" all three times John uses it of Jesus here because of its emphasis as a definite article. Jesus is not just another word. Jesus is THE one and only Word of God, who was God and with God in the beginning.

"In the beginning" (Genesis 1:1), creation was occurring. But Jesus was not created. In fact, John goes on to declare: *"Through Him (Jesus) all things were made; without Him nothing was made that has been made"* (John 1:3 NIV). Jesus is Creator God.

But the best news is that Jesus is not some far off, aloof God—powerful enough to create but too removed and remote to understand our concerns and feel what we feel. The truth is that Jesus refuses to stay away from us. His love for us makes us too irresistible.

Check out how John brings his introduction of Jesus to a climax: *"THE Word became flesh and dwelt among us, and we have seen His glory, glory as of the only Son from the Father, full of grace and truth!"* (John 1:14 ESV).

At the end of our forty days with Jesus, I want us to be able to say with John, *"We have seen His glory, glory as of the only Son from the Father, full of grace and truth!"*

Today is day one! Let's get "I AM" crazy!

Today's Crazy Big Idea: Jesus is God who became human to be our help and hope!

Today's Crazy Scripture: *"For God so loved the world that He gave His one and only Son, that whoever believes in Him should not perish but have eternal life!"* (John 3:16 NIV).

Today's Crazy Prayer Starter: "Lord Jesus, please open my mind and my heart to receive all that You want to reveal to me. I want to experience Your glory in my life. I humble myself before You. I am ready to learn from You. In Your name I pray, Amen!"

"I AM" CRAZY

I've got a story for you; a true story, a famous story. It's a Jesus story that powerfully piles up the proof, so you can believe Jesus is God; so you can believe Jesus Himself when He repeatedly claimed to be God; so you can understand why they killed Jesus because He would not stop claiming to be God; so you can celebrate Jesus as God in His victory over death; so you can worship Jesus right now, rightly exalted as Lord of lords and King of kings.

I want to show you this story because I want to showcase what it means for you that Jesus is God. It means when you're hurting, He has the healing. It means when you're in a bad place, He can get you to a better place. It means when you have a problem, He has a promise to fix it. When you have a need, He has a Name to meet your deepest need, your every need.

Okay, here's the story. It takes place way back in Exodus, the second book of the Bible. You know the main character of this story. His name is Moses. Moses may be the main character of the story, but he is not the star of the story. The star of the story is Jesus. With Jesus as the star of the story, Moses' life goes in a whole new direction; from nothing to something very special. Moses has an experience of the supernatural presence and power of God. That's what happens to everyone who lets Jesus be the star of their story. When Jesus becomes the star of your story, He changes everything.

Here's what happens to Moses when Jesus becomes the star of his story: *"Now Moses was tending the flock of Jethro, his father-in-law..."* (Exodus 3:1 NIV).

Immediately, two insights rise to the surface of the story. First, Moses is really poor. Shepherds were of the lowest class of people. These weren't even his sheep. They belonged to his father-in-law. Moses has nothing to his name. But here's what's more and what's worse. Moses is convinced he is nothing and deserves to have nothing.

Have you ever been there? Have you ever felt like you deserve the bad stuff that happens to you because of bad stuff you had done in your past. That's Moses.

The second insight we gain is from the Hebrew word for "tending." It means "feeding." Moses is just doing his job—what shepherds do. He's just going about his ordinary, day-in and day-out business, getting the sheep to a place where they can feed.

"He led the flock to the far side of the desert and came to Horeb, the mountain of God" (Exodus 3:1 NIV).

Moses knew he wanted to get his sheep to Horeb. There was water and vegetation there. What Moses did not know was that God was there. Not only was God present in that place; God had drawn Moses to that place.

This is exactly what God is making His best effort to do in your life. Just as you're going about your ordinary business, God wants to draw you to Himself. God has a holy place to which He is drawing you, so He can do in you what He did in Moses.

Here's the lesson Moses is about to learn that the Lord wants to teach us: **God draws us to Himself in order to draw us out of ourselves!**

What does this mean? Like Moses, we can be our own worst enemies. God draws us to Himself to draw us out of our self-absorption; to draw us out of our low self-worth; to draw us out of our insecurities; to draw us out of our self-pity; to draw us out of our fears; to draw us out of our shame. God draws us to Himself to draw us out of ourselves and set us free—free of doubt and guilt; free of stress and worry.

Right now, I believe you are being drawn to your mountain of God. Before this day is over, I pray you find yourself saying what a guy named Jacob said: *"God is in this place—truly. And I didn't even know it!"* (Genesis 28:16 MSG).

Here's how it happened to Moses. *"There the Angel of the LORD appeared to him in flames of fire from within a bush. Moses saw that though the bush was on fire, it did not burn up. So Moses thought, 'I will go over and see this strange sight—why the bush does not burn up'"* (Exodus 3:2,3 NIV).

Here's a second lesson we can learn with Moses: **When God draws us to Himself, we meet the angel of the LORD!**

Who is the Angel of the LORD? This is not the only time this heavenly Person shows up in Scripture. Approximately 70 times, the Bible mentions the Angel of the LORD and every time, He is strikingly similar to Jesus. In fact, I believe the Angel of the LORD is Jesus before He comes to earth through human birth—what theologians call the "pre-existent Christ."

"I AM" CRAZY

My point is not to do an in-depth study on this issue. But let me give you a top ten list of evidences that the Angel of the LORD is Jesus.

1. He is understood to be the LORD! (Genesis 16:10; John 14:9; 20:28)
2. He speaks as if He is the LORD! (Judges 2:1,2; John 10:30)
3. He is sent from the Father! (Judges 13:9; John 6:38; 8:42)
4. He speaks with the authority of God, giving commands. (Judges 13:12-14; Matthew 7:28,29; 8:27; 28:18)
5. He forgives sins. (Zechariah 3:3,4: Matthew 9:2)
6. He is seen as the Commander of the LORD's army. (Joshua 5:14; Revelation 19:11-14)
7. He allows people to worship him as the LORD! (Judges 16:19-21; Matthew 28:9)
8. He offers the comfort of the LORD! (I Kings 19:3-8; Matthew 11:28-30)
9. He makes promises only the LORD can make! (Genesis 16:10; John 14:1-3)
10. He refers to himself as "I AM!" (Exodus 3:14; John 8:58)

The best thing that could happen to you today is to have a person-to-person encounter with Jesus. At one time, He appeared through history as the Angel of the LORD. Now He's trying to draw you to Himself. He's trying to grab your full attention. He sees you in your need. He wants to reveal who He is to you and what He can do for you.

DAY 2

Today's Crazy Big Idea: Jesus wants to draw you to Himself to draw you out of yourself!

Today's Crazy Scripture: *"God is in this place—truly. And I didn't even know it!"* (Genesis 28:16 MSG).

Today's Crazy Prayer Starter: "Lord Jesus, you have my full attention. Thank You for drawing me to yourself. Lord, I want to be drawn out of myself, free of all that limits my life—free of my fears and worries, free of my guilt and shame, free to know You and love You. I open myself right now to an experience of Your peace and Your presence. Please help me find You and feel You here in this moment. In Your Name, Amen!"

"I AM" CRAZY

Here's the crazy question I have leftover from Day 2: Why is the Angel of the LORD appearing to Moses out of a bush, of all things? I mean, this is the God of the universe after all. Why not make an appearance in a tornado or an earthquake? Why a bush?

Let's consider this: If we dig deeper than the English, we find that the Hebrew word used here in the original text means more than bush. It means thorn bush. What's the significance of this? It points my heart to Jesus, wearing a crown of thorns. The LORD shows up in what would be a symbol of His suffering for my sin (Matthew 27:29).

This is a picture of Jesus and His willingness to make whatever sacrifice is necessary to seek us out and save us, even when we don't know how lost we are (Luke 15; 19:9,10).

Jesus used a thorn bush to draw the attention of Moses, to draw him out of himself—out of his self-pity; out of his self-absorption. What is Jesus using to draw your attention?

It's probably not a thorn bush. He did that once. Jesus is so creative that He rarely does the same thing twice. But know this: Jesus is definitely trying to draw your attention, to draw you out of yourself—to draw you out of your pain and problems. What do you think Jesus might be using in your life to draw your attention to Himself?

Here's what happened with Moses. *"When the LORD saw that he had gone over to look, God called to him from within the bush, 'Moses! Moses!'"* (Exodus 3:4 NIV).

Whatever the LORD is using to call you to Himself and out of yourself is your burning bush. This is the holy place where God longs to speak into your life. It may be this book you're reading. It may be a health issue, a financial issue, or a parenting issue. Whatever it is, embrace it. When you give the Lord your full attention, He takes His engagement with your life to another level.

I love how Moses responded to the LORD's call: *"Moses said, 'Here I am!'"* (Exodus 3:4).

These three words can change everything. When you make yourself available to God—"Here I am!"—it opens the door to Him to give you a purpose you never had before; to give you a power you never had before; to give you His presence like never before. Here's how it happened to Moses: *"'Do not come any closer,' God said. 'Take off your sandals, for the place where you are standing is holy ground!'"* (Exodus 3:5 NIV).

The word "holy" means "set apart for God's purpose"—set apart for God's dream.

When you make yourself fully available to God—"Here I am!"—you put yourself in the place where He can reveal His dream for your life. You get to meet the Lord of eternity. You get to move into His purpose for your life. You get to experience God shaping you into His best version of you.

Notice that before Moses could step onto holy ground, he had to remove his sandals. Is there something you need to strip out of your life, so you step into His holy presence; so you can step into His dream for your life? Once Moses was obedient to the LORD by removing his sandals, he got to meet His God like he never had before.

"And He said, 'I am the God of your father, the God of Abraham, the God of Isaac and the God of Jacob.' At this, Moses hid his face because he was afraid to look at God" (Exodus 3:6 NIV).

Abraham lived 700 years before Moses. This is the God of eternity. This is the God of generations. Isaac was Abraham's son. Jacob was the grandson of Abraham. But this is very personal to Moses because this is the God of his own father.

This is how the LORD wants you to know Him—unlimited God, unbounded God, forever God. But He is not far off God. He's the God who comes close and draws you to Himself. This up-close God longs to have a deeply personal relationship with you. He wants you to know He knows you inside and out. He is profoundly concerned about everything in your life—large and small. If it matters to you, it matters to your LORD!

This is how the LORD revealed His heart to Moses: *"The LORD said, 'I have indeed seen the misery of My people in Egypt. I have heard them crying out because of their slave drivers, and I am concerned about their suffering. So I have come down to rescue them...'"* (Exodus 3:7,8 NIV).

I know these verses are written about God's people, the nation of Israel. But when God said them to Moses, I think Moses personalized them for himself. I think Moses felt it in his soul: "God has seen my misery. God has heard the cry of my heart. God has come down to rescue me." I believe this because Moses would later write this: *"In the desert land He found him, in a barren and howling waste. He shielded him and cared for him; He guarded him as the apple of His eye"* (Deuteronomy 32:10 NIV).

It's important that you personalize this as well. Get this truth anchored in your soul—God has found you in your barren, howling waste. A deeply caring God guards and shields you because He loves you beyond your wildest dreams. Can you get that?

Moses got the love of the Lord. You can get it, too. Do you believe God loves everyone? Of course. That's easy to believe. Do you know what's harder to believe? God loves you. Do you believe God loves you? God's love for you is an ever-seeing love; an ever-hearing love; an ever-caring love. You are the apple of His eye!

Today's Crazy Big Idea: Jesus is willing to seek us out and save us, even when we don't know how lost we are.

Today's Crazy Scripture: *"In the desert land He found him, in a barren and howling waste. He shielded him and cared for him. He guarded him as the apple of His eye"* (Deuteronomy 32:10 NIV).

Today's Crazy Prayer Starter: "Dear LORD, here I am! I want to be found by You. I want to find Your dream for my life. I am so grateful that You love and care for me. Help me to grasp the height and the depth and the length and the breadth of Your love for me. Please be my Shield, and guard me as the apple of Your eye. Help me strip away from my life anything that hinders my relationship with You. In Your Name, Amen!"

"I AM" CRAZY

"I AM" CRAZY
DAY 4

"Misery loves company!" So the old saying goes. Does this mean miserable people want to hang out with other miserable people? Does it mean that miserable people look for comfort in the company of others—miserable or not? Neither are very good options.

Here's our LORD's hope for us when our lives move into misery: *"They will seek My face - in their misery they will earnestly seek Me"* (Hosea 5:15 NIV).

Here's the LORD's rock-solid promise to those who earnestly seek Him: *"You will call upon Me and come and pray to Me, and I will listen to you. You will seek Me and find Me. When you seek Me with all of your heart, I will be found by you,' declares the LORD"* (Jeremiah 29:12-14 NIV).

Whatever it is—whoever it is—that makes your life miserable, your LORD is longing to be found. So know this: **When we have a hurt, the LORD has a heart!**

The LORD has a huge heart of compassion. Here's what's awesome: the LORD'S compassion always takes action to rescue, deliver, and save. On Day 3, we learned that the LORD God would not leave His people in their pain. He will not leave you in yours.

Today, let's look again at what Jesus said from the burning thorn bush because His words project a picture of why He died for us on the cross.

"I have indeed seen the misery of My people...I have heard them crying out because of their (sin). I am concerned about their suffering. So I have come down to rescue them" (Exodus 3:7,8 NIV).

Imagine Jesus speaking these very words to you personally from the cross. Paul put it this way: *"God demonstrates His own love for us in this: While we were still sinners, Christ died for us!"* (Romans 5:8 NIV).

In His conversation with Moses, the LORD goes on to describe what His rescue will look like. *"I have come down to rescue them from the hand of the Egyptians and to bring them up out of that land into a good and spacious land, a land flowing with milk and honey!"* (Exodus 3:8 NIV).

This is not just a story about a people long, long ago. This story is a right now story for people like us. **When we're in a bad place, God's got a better place!**

When you're in a bad place—whether it's your marriage, your job, your parenting, your finances, your health, your emotions—Jesus wants to do more than get you out of the bad place. He wants to elevate your life; lift you up on the higher ground of abundant living. Guess what? Your Jesus is able to do immeasurably more, abundantly more than all you ask or imagine according to His power at work in you (Ephesians 3:20).

How can I be so confident and assured? I know the end of the story. I know what the LORD did for Moses. I know what He did for His people. Most importantly, I know what He's done for me—how He's taken my marriage, my ministry, my money, and emotions out of a really bad place. I know how He continues to make my life better and better. He's fully forgiven me and redeemed me from the pit of my own sin, crowned me with love and compassion, and satisfied my desires with good things (Psalm 103:3-5).

In our text, Jesus is showing Himself to Moses and to us as a good God! But He's got even more in store. *"Now the cry of the Israelites has reached Me and I have seen the way the Egyptians are oppressing them. So now I am sending you to Pharaoh to bring My people, the Israelites, out of Egypt!"* (Exodus 3:9,10 NIV).

The LORD is promising Moses what I've just been telling you is His specialty. He will take Moses from leading a bunch of sheep to leading a nation of people. He will take Moses from the desert wasteland to the palace of the king. Moses will be set free to live out God's dream for his life.

However, Moses feels totally inadequate to take on the LORD'S dream for his life. In fact, Moses begins to protest, "Lord, you've got the wrong guy. I'm a loser. I'm nobody. I've screwed up everything I've ever tried to do. I'm nothing—nothing but a failure."

The LORD says, "Moses, get over yourself": *"God said, 'I will be with you. And this will be a sign to you that it is I who have sent you. When you have brought the people out of Egypt, you will worship God on this mountain!"* (Exodus 3:12 NIV).

The LORD is saying to Moses and to each of us, "You do what I say, and I'm going work things out beyond your wildest dreams. I'm going to be so good to you, all you'll want to do is fall down and give Me praise, worship, and heart-felt thanks."

What's the biggest thing God has ever asked you to do? What's the biggest gift God has ever asked you to give? What's

"I AM" CRAZY

the biggest step of faith He's ever asked you to take? Where is He asking you to step out in faith right now? How are you responding to the LORD of your burning bush?

Satan keeps trying to lead you back into your slavery to sin. Jesus keeps trying to bring you back to the mountain of God. How are you responding?

Here's how Moses responded. *"Moses said to God, 'Suppose I go to the Israelites and say to them, The God of your fathers has sent me to you,' and they ask me, 'What's His name?' Then what shall I tell them?'"* (Exodus 3:13 NIV).

Moses goes from thinking he's not good enough to thinking God's not good enough. The LORD has a plan for miraculously working everything together for the good. How can Moses trust the plan if He does not trust the God of the plan? Have you ever been there? Have you ever found it difficult to trust God's plan for your marriage, for your children, for your finances, for your future? Have you ever wanted to cry out with Moses, "Who are You, God?"

Here's what the LORD said to Moses: **"I am I AM!"** (Exodus 3:14 NIV). The LORD is not stuttering. He is declaring His name. "I AM" is "Yahweh" in Hebrew. To Moses, this name would mean "the One who causes to be."

"This is what you are to say to the Israelites, 'I AM has sent me to you…This is My name forever, the name by which I am to be remembered…'" (Exodus 3:14,15 NIV).

So now we know what Jesus actually meant every time He made an "I AM" declaration. He was announcing that He was God—as much God as God the Father is God—the God who causes to be. He was creating a new burning bush experience for all who would be drawn to Him. What is the burning bush experience Jesus is calling you to right now? Maybe today you're standing on holy ground, where the LORD reveals Himself as the great "I AM" and longs to reveal His great dream for your life.

Today's Crazy Big Idea: When we're in a bad place, God's got a better place!

Today's Crazy Scripture: *"'For I know the plans I have for you,' declares the LORD, 'plans to prosper you and not to harm you, plans to give you hope and a future. Then you will call upon Me and come and pray to Me, and I will listen to you. You will seek Me and find Me. When you seek Me with all your heart, I will be found by you,' declares the LORD"* (Jeremiah 29:11-14 NIV).

Today's Crazy Prayer Starter: "Dear Lord, thank You for caring about my life. Thank You for caring enough to listen to my prayer. I'm seeking You with all my heart. Thank You for being a God who wants to be found. I want to know You, Lord, as You want to be known. Please reveal Yourself to me. I need You, Lord. In Jesus' name, Amen!

"I AM" CRAZY

"I AM" CRAZY
DAY 5

So far in our journey, we have watched as the eternal, pre-existent Jesus drew Moses to Himself. In today's story, Jesus does not draw anybody. He is drawn to somebody—an anonymous somebody. We don't even know her name. This is good news for us. If Jesus is drawn to an anonymous anybody, that means He can be drawn to you and me.

Today's story is about a person in the depths of hopelessness. She is a woman who has nothing left to live for; a woman who knows only rejection and shame. She doesn't know it, but today's her day to have a life-changing encounter. She is about to meet Someone who will turn her blasé, black and white world to brilliant Technicolor in 4K ultra HD. As it is, she's given up hope of anything beyond mere survival. She has no idea that Jesus is being irresistibly drawn to her.

When our story opens, we find her walking a hot, dusty dirt path to the village, well under the blistering heat of the noonday, middle-eastern sun. What's so crazy and so sad is that nobody goes to the well for water when the sun is at its hottest. Women would go to the well every day. It was the social high point of the day—singing, sharing gossip, and laughing. But

"I AM" CRAZY

they go for water at the crack of dawn when the day is pleasantly cool. This woman goes at noon because, if she goes in the morning, she is the butt of every joke; she is the target of every hurtful, unkind word. Even little kids throw sticks and clods of manure at her. So she goes at noon.

What she does not know is that as she makes her way to the well, Jesus makes His way to her. Just as right at this moment, Jesus is making His way to you.

At the time of our story, Jesus is 30 years old. He's recently been baptized by John the Baptist. We know the ultimate end of the story. We know that Jesus is the Son of God. But guess who's the very first person Jesus actually tells that He's God in the flesh? It's this woman, who is racially different than Jesus; who practices a strange religion.

I want to know what draws Jesus to this woman; what moves Jesus to reveal Himself to this woman, because I want Jesus to be drawn to me; to reveal Himself to me.

This woman doesn't even see Jesus coming. Is that you? Are you only a heartbeat away? A prayer away from Jesus showing up and showing off in your life?

What has her blinded actually is what blinds us. She is blinded by her brokenness.

This woman has been beaten and broken so many times in so many ways. She has been married and divorced five times. Presently, she's living with a man who will take her to his bed but won't give her his name. She feels like damaged goods—a woman easily thrown away.

From research I've done of primitive pagan culture, I don't think this woman is like the town floozy. I think she struggles with infertility. She cannot get pregnant. She can get married, but once married, she cannot make a baby. Man after man booted her out. "You can cook and clean. But if you can't give me a child, I can't have you. I won't have you. I divorce you. I divorce you. I divorce you. Away with you." Those searing words had scorched her soul five times by five different men. Her clothes are thrown out the door, and she's on the street. She is not loved for who she is. She's cast aside for what she can't produce. Because she's a non-producer, she feels like a non-person.

Here's the big question. What is it in this broken woman that draws Jesus irresistibly to show up and show off in her life? In that culture, she is the wrong gender. Women were treated more like pieces of property than persons. But that's Jesus. He always looks for opportunities to honor and elevate women.

But this woman is also the wrong race. And that's another thing about Jesus. It is not that He is racially colorblind. Jesus celebrates every different race as unique, beautiful and of distinctive value to Him.

Okay, but this woman is of the wrong religion. Her ideas about God are all messed up.

But Jesus is drawn to her like she's Mother Teresa.

Do you know what it is about this woman that makes her so attractive to Jesus? It's her brokenness. This is good news for all of us because there's something painfully messed up in each one of us. Maybe you want to protest, "Not me—I'm all good." But here's the truth: there is something messed up in everything and everyone because of sin.

There's something messed up in every government and every school because of sin. There's something messed up in every business and industry because of sin. There's something messed up in every family and friendship because of sin. There's something messed up in you. There's something messed up in me because of sin. The good news is it's our brokenness that makes us irresistible to Jesus.

In fact, at our church we like to say it this way: "I'm a mess. You're a mess. Let's get our messes closer to Jesus!"

David writes it this way in a song: *"The LORD is close to the brokenhearted and saves those who are crushed in spirit!"* (Psalm 34:18 NIV).

This is why God the Father sent His Son, Jesus, to our planet. *"The Spirit of the Sovereign LORD…has sent Me to bind up the broken…"* (Isaiah 61:1 NIV).

And this is exactly why Jesus is drawn to you!

Today's Crazy Big Idea: It's our brokenness that makes us irresistible to Jesus.

Today's Crazy Scripture: *"He heals the brokenhearted and binds up their wounds"* (Psalms 147:3 NIV).

Today's Crazy Prayer Starter: "Dear Lord, I am so grateful that when I'm at my ugliest, You find me the most attractive. Thank You for not leaving me in my brokenness. You are my Healer, my Helper, my Hope. I give you praise for not giving up on me. In the name of Jesus, Amen."

"I AM" CRAZY

"I AM" CRAZY
DAY 6

How does Jesus do His healing, binding work for people who are broken? We can see how He does it for the woman in our story. While this broken woman is on her way to the well, Jesus is making a beeline for her. Here's how John describes the encounter.

"The Pharisees heard that Jesus was gaining and baptizing more disciples than John, although in fact it was not Jesus who baptized, but His disciples. When the Lord learned of this, He left Judea and went back once more to Galilee" (John 4:1-3 NIV).

The first thing I want us to see here is what Jesus is not drawn to—what He is repulsed by. John finds it important, as he opens this story, to show Jesus making a strong move away from religion. The religious leaders were keeping score and making comparisons. That's what religious people do. "We're more right than you. We're more holy than you. God blesses us more than you." Jesus wanted as far from that nastiness as He could get.

Jesus likes to get as much distance as possible between Himself and religion. Jesus has such a passion for broken people. He's always trying to get as close as possible to people in pain. Nothing and no one can keep Jesus from getting to broken people.

Look how John describes it: *"Now Jesus had to go through Samaria"* (John 4:4 NIV).

What? No self-respecting Jew would go through Samaria. Jews always took the long way around Samaria. It was not safe. Jews and Samaritans despised each other. They were different races and practiced different religions. Not much has changed in that part of the world in the past 2000 years.

But the text says, *"Jesus had to ..."* Jesus is God. He does not have to do anything He does not want to do. But when we dig deeper than the English, we see that in John's original Greek the force of the language is emphatic: "Jesus had to had to ..." I like to read it this way: "It was an absolute necessity for Jesus to go through Samaria."

Jesus was not taking a shortcut. For Jesus, it was an absolute necessity to get to this woman in her brokenness by the most direct route.

Jesus will catch up with this woman as she's going about her everyday business. That's what He's trying to do with you. Jesus is keenly aware of what you've been through and what you're going through. Jesus sees it as an absolute necessity for Him to join you in the stress and struggle of your everyday business.

Before we read more of the story, we've got to put ourselves in the story. This woman is me. This woman is you. Jesus will do everything in His power to get to us when we're hurting. *"So Jesus came into Sychar, a Samaritan village ...Jesus, worn out by the trip, sat down at the well. It was noon"* (John 4:5,6 MSG).

Jesus is so determined to make a difference in this woman's life, He exhausts Himself to put Himself right in her path at just the right time to meet with her.

"A woman, a Samaritan, came to draw water" (John 4:7 MSG). What would be normal for any other Jewish man would be to get up and get as far away from the woman as possible. But there's nothing normal about Jesus. He invites her closer.

"Jesus said, 'Would you give Me a drink of water?' The Samaritan woman, taken aback, asked, 'How come you, a Jew, are asking me a Samaritan woman for a drink?' (Jews in those days would not be caught dead talking to Samaritans)" (John 4:7-9 MSG).

Do you know what I love about this? Jesus is not afraid of nor put off by our messes. Jesus is not a clean freak. He loves to get His hands dirty, bringing beauty out of our brokenness. Our mess is like a magnet that draws Him to us. In fact, when we are at our absolute worst, Jesus offers us His absolute best.

That's what He does for the woman. *"Jesus said, 'If you knew the generosity of God and who I am, you would be asking Me for a drink, and I would give you fresh, living water'"* (John 4:10 MSG).

This is not just a story about Jesus and a broken woman a long time ago. This is a right now story about you and Jesus. He's offering you living water for your inner ache. It's a healing water. It's the cure of Christ for every crisis you'll ever go through.

When pain punctures our hearts, our joy is the first thing to leak out. This living water is a generous gift from a lavishly giving God to bring fresh joy into your life. Gifts are given for our enjoyment. It's the joyous gift of being cleansed of all guilt and shame.

Jesus is offering you this living water to fill your inner emptiness. This water is restorative. It satisfies your deepest desires. You take a deep drink of this water, and it restores God's best version of you. When Jesus offers you and this woman this fresh, living water, He's offering new life.

The problem is we all have a history of drinking from the wrong well. Here's how God said it: *"My people have committed two sins: They have forsaken Me, the spring of Living Water, and have dug their own cisterns, broken cisterns that cannot hold water"* (Jeremiah 2:13 NIV).

Just like we all have done, this woman has been trying to satisfy her soul by drinking out of broken wells—wells that won't even hold water. She's not yet ready to trust Jesus.

Have you been there? Have you gone to the wrong well and come up empty? You were hoping money would satisfy. But you came up empty. You were hoping marriage would satisfy. But you came up empty. You were hoping the right house, the right job, the right retirement would satisfy. Empty! Empty! Life gets painfully empty when you go to the wrong well long enough. Are you ready to truly trust Jesus with your emptiness?

Today's Crazy Big Idea: Jesus sees it as an absolute necessity to join you in your pain.

Today's Crazy Scripture: *"If you knew the generosity of God and who I AM, you would be asking Me for a drink, and I would give your fresh, living water"* (John 4:10 MSG).

Today's Crazy Prayer Starter: "Dear Lord, I am tired of my emptiness. I'm sorry for neglecting You. I'm sorry for trying to satisfy my soul on stuff that doesn't matter and will not last. I thirst for You, Lord. I know You are good. I know You can be trusted. Please let me drink of Your fresh, living water. In Your saving name, Amen!

"I AM" CRAZY

"I AM" CRAZY
DAY 7

Everyone has trust issues. It's only a matter of whether the issues are big or small. Moses had big trust issues from the damage he had done to himself. His guilt and shame kept him from trusting the LORD, the LORD's plan, and the LORD's promises. Moses' lack of trust created a gap in his life, separating him from any sense of hope or peace or joy or purpose. The LORD bridged that "trust" gap with His Name—"I am I AM! "I AM with you! "I AM your God! I AM your hope of the miraculous!"

Once Moses let go of his trust issues, the LORD took hold of him and the miraculous began to flow in and through his life. What was true for Moses is true for you and me. And it was true for this broken woman by the well. She had big trust issues from the damage that had been done to her. Can you relate?

Here's what the woman said to Jesus when He invites her to trust Him by offering her a drink of living water: *"The woman said, 'Sir, you don't even have a bucket to draw with and this well is deep! So how are you going to get this living water?'"* (John 4:11 MSG).

What I love about Jesus is that even when we resist Him, He won't give up on us. Pointing at the well, *"Jesus said, 'Everyone who drinks this water will get thirsty again and again. Anyone who drinks the water I give will never thirst—not ever. The water I give will be an artesian spring within, gushing fountains of endless life!"* (John 4:13,14 MSG).

Notice the words "everyone" and "anyone." Everyone drinks from the wrong well—the broken well that never satisfies. But anyone can receive the free gift of Jesus' living water. Anyone. Anyone can be you. You can receive a fresh, new life from Jesus.

The woman wanted to be anyone. *"She said, 'Sir, give me this water, so I won't ever get thirsty, won't ever have to come back to this well again!'"* (John 4:15 NIV).

She wants to be done with her old broken life and its pain. She wants a less stressful, new life. But that's a problem. Jesus does not so much want to relieve her stress as He wants to rescue her soul. So He does for her what He does for us when He wants to heal us of our painful past. Jesus cares enough to confront her with her sin.

"Jesus told her, 'Go, call your husband and come back.' 'I have no husband,' she replied. Jesus said to her, 'You are right when you say you have no husband. The fact is, you have had five husbands, and the man you now have is not your husband'" (John 4:16-18 NIV).

Do you know what I love about this brief, but intense, interaction? In as gentle a way as possible, Jesus helps her face the truth of her life. Jesus knows that denial is deadly. He cares enough to confront, but Jesus refuses to condemn.

What was good news for the woman is good news for us. *"God did not go to all the trouble of sending His Son merely to point an accusing finger, telling people how bad they are. He came to help people get right with God. Anyone who trusts in Jesus is not condemned!"* (John 4:17,18 MSG, DCV).

Do you know why this is true? Though we each deserve to be condemned for our sin, Jesus took upon Himself all the condemnation due us, when He died for our sins on the cross. He was our substitute and took our place and got the punishment we deserved.

When Jesus refuses to condemn the woman, though He knows all the truth about her broken life, notice how she opens up to Him spiritually. *"'Sir,' the woman said, 'I can see that you are a prophet!' 'Woman,' Jesus replied, 'believe Me …A time is coming and has now come when true worshippers will worship the Father in Spirit and in truth!'"* (John 4:21,23 NIV).

Jesus points to His Heavenly Father as the ultimate solution to every struggle. This creates a great spiritual thirst in the woman for the possible coming of Christ the King. *"The woman said, 'I know that Christ is coming. When He comes, He will explain everything to us!'"* (John 4:25 NIV).

Jesus now reveals Himself to her just as He revealed Himself to Moses—just as He wants to reveal Himself to you. *"Then Jesus declared, 'I, the One speaking to you—I AM He!'"* (John 4:26 NIV).

In the Greek text, the pronoun "He" is not present. It's simply added to make sense to our English ears. What Jesus actually said is, *'I, the One speaking to you—I AM!'"* Jesus uses the same name of Himself with this woman that He used with Moses. In the Greek it's "Ego Eimi"; in the Hebrew it's "Yahweh." Either way, it is Jesus claiming to be God, the great "I AM!"

She knew without a doubt that Jesus was claiming to be the Christ, the Son of the living God, as much God as God is God. She trusted Him and wanted others to trust Him too.

"Then, leaving her water jar, the woman went back to the town and said to the people, 'Come, see a man, who told me everything I ever did. Could this be the Christ?' They came out of the town and made their way to Jesus!" (John 4:28-30 NIV).

She comes to the well empty, angry, and miserable with all the pain of her past. But the great "I AM" was waiting for her with the possibility of new life. All she had to do was trust Jesus enough to accept a drink of His fresh, living water. She took a big sip and ran from that well, forgetting her water jar and what brought her there in the first place. She had something—Someone—new alive inside her; alive with hope and joy and love. This was news too good to keep to herself.

Jesus is waiting for you right now, just as He was waiting for the woman. He is still the great "I AM!" He's still making a sensational offer—a gushing fountain of eternal life.

Today's Crazy Big Idea: When I trust the LORD, He shows me His plan and gives me His promises!

Today's Crazy Scripture: *"God didn't go to all the trouble of sending His Son merely to point an accusing finger, telling people how bad they are. He came to help people get right with God. Anyone who trusts in Jesus is not condemned"* (John 3:17,18 MSG).

Today's Crazy Prayer Starter: "Dear Jesus, thank You for refusing to condemn me. I know I'm a sinner and I need you. I trust You. Please help me trust You more. Amen.

"I AM" CRAZY

"I AM" CRAZY
DAY 8

Jesus calls you into this crazy spiritual adventure because He wants to do more than just have you read a book. Jesus is calling you to hope. He's calling you out of worry and fear into hope. He's calling you out of being stressed and over busy into hope. Jesus is calling you out of the chaos and confusion of life and into His living hope.

Hearing Jesus calling you to hope has such huge implications for getting your life to a better place in all respects. So I pray this scripture for you every day: *"I pray ...that you may know the hope to which the Lord has called you!"* (Ephesians 1:18 NIV).

The word "know" here refers to an experiential knowledge. You have to experience it to actually know it. Jesus is calling you to experience unshakeable hope.

Do you know how Jesus calls you to hope? He does so by revealing Himself to you. This is why we're studying the "I AM" statements. Every time Jesus makes a definitive declaration about Himself, He's trying to reveal who He is to you and the hope He longs to be for you. "I AM the Bread of Life!" "I AM the Good Shepherd!" "I AM the Light of the World!" "I

AM the Way, the Truth and the Life!" "I AM the Resurrection and the Life!" "I AM the Door!" With each "I AM" statement, Jesus is calling you to hope.

But before Jesus can get you to see your hope, He has to get you out of your blinding darkness. I say "blinding" darkness because it's your darkness that blinds you to hope.

Here's the first big question: Where are things starting to go dark in your life—at work, at home, in your thinking, in the way you feel? Where has darkness crept into your life?

Here's the second question: When did the darkness start to settle over your life? Was it when you got some really bad news from your doctor? Was it when someone you love dearly found out that the cancer is terminal? Has darkness settled over a friendship that seems to be slipping away? Has your parenting gone all dark?

I don't know where or when life began to go dark for you. But I know this: Jesus is calling you to hope. Here's the really good news. When you respond to His call, Jesus makes hope happen!

I want hope to happen in your life, so I'm going to take you into a story. But to get to hope, we've got to do more than read this story; we've got to step into it and feel it and know it by experience. Here we go.

"By now it was dark, and Jesus had not yet joined them" (John 6:17 NIV).

These are the close friends of Jesus. He had told them to get in a boat and sail to the other side of the lake. He'd see them later.

Did He mean later He would join them in the boat, or later He would somehow meet them on the other side? They did not know. They were not sure. They waited as long as they could for Jesus, but now it was dark. When it got good and dark, they kept asking each other, "Where's Jesus?"

Have you ever wanted to know the answer to that question for your life? When your marriage gets good and dark, where's Jesus? When financial issues or health issues or job issues have your life in the dark, where's Jesus?

I can tell you where He is. Jesus is where He always is. When your life begins to get dark and you're looking for Jesus, He's in the very same place He was when it started to get dark for a boat-load of His followers. When Jesus knows darkness is coming our way, He goes into prayer on our behalf.

Matthew tells us that's exactly what Jesus was doing, while His followers were waiting in the dark. *"After Jesus had dismissed them, He went up on a mountainside by Himself to pray!"* (Matthew 14:23 NIV).

I love this image because I need to know where Jesus is when my life goes dark. Have you ever wondered that? You're in a dark time relationally, a dark time mentally and emotionally, and your heart cries out, "Where are You, Jesus?" Now you know where He is. He's far above you, praying for you.

Here's how the Bible describes it: *"Jesus lives forever. He has a permanent priesthood. Therefore He is able to save completely those who come to God through Him, because He always lives to pray for them!"* (Hebrews 7:24,25 NIV).

So from His lofty perspective, as Jesus prays for the guys in the boat, He sees everything that's happening to them, everything they're going through. He sees them in the dark. This is not because Jesus is wearing some high-tech night vision goggles; this is because Jesus is God. One of His names is El Roi, the God who sees.

Here's how it worked for His followers in the boat: *"Jesus saw the disciples straining at the oars, because the wind was against them"* (Mark 6:48 NIV).

Where does it feel like life has aligned itself against you? Where are you straining? When you're under emotional strain and mental strain; when there's a strain on your marriage or a strain on your finances; when you're under severe physical strain or job strain, do you ever say to yourself, "I'm not going to make it. We're not going to make it"? I think that's the kind of hopeless fear that gripped the disciples in their boat.

The disciples didn't know it. But they were in for a Christ-glorified experience. All they were feeling at the moment was the strain. There's only one sure remedy when life feels like a strain. It's a glorified remedy. *"Christ in you the hope of glory!"* (Colossians 1:27 NIV). Christ in your marriage is the hope for a glorified marriage. Christ in your parenting is the hope of glorified parenting. Christ in your life is the hope of a glorified life.

Today's Crazy Big Idea: Jesus is calling you to hope!

Today's Crazy Scripture: *"Christ in you the hope of glory!"* (Colossians 1:27 NIV).

Today's Crazy Prayer Starter: "Dear Lord, please help me to experience the hope to which you have called me. Even when darkness starts to settle over my life; when everything seems to go against me, I know you can make my life glorious. Amen."

"I AM" CRAZY

"I AM" CRAZY
DAY 9

"The boat was far out to sea, when the wind came up against them and they were battered by the waves!" (Matthew 14:24 MSG).

Have you ever had a crisis go from bad to worse? That's what's happening to the boys in the boat. First, they're trying to navigate through the darkness, just like we keep trying to find our way when life goes dark. Then the wind comes up against them. They're straining at the oars while their boat's being battered by the waves. I can just hear them screaming, "We're not going to make it!"

It is said that the darkest hour is just before the dawn. That's what happens to the boys in the boat. They've been battling the wind and the waves for hours. They don't think they are going to make it. Look what happens. *"About the fourth watch of the night, Jesus went out to them, walking on the lake!"* (Mark 6:48 NIV).

By the military terms of that day, the fourth watch of the night began at 3 a.m. The boys in the boat had been struggling. They started their trip across the Sea of Galilee in the first watch of the night. They probably had a sail up. In the second watch of the night, the sail was down because the wind was against them. At midnight and for the next three hours, during the third watch of the night, they were soaking wet, trying to bail water as their little craft was taking a pounding from wicked waves. Just when they had given up hope; when they had done everything in their power to save themselves; when they didn't think they were going to make it, Jesus comes to them in the storm.

I love this part. It affirms a life truth I've learned in all my personal storms. There's no storm so severe as to keep Jesus away. But I have a question. Why does Jesus wait until the fourth watch of the night to do some gravity-defying wave-walking? Why does He save His miracle for what seems like a last-second rescue? What's up with that?

I think the answer might be hidden in the prayers Jesus was praying on the mountain-side before He walked on water. Jesus is praying for His followers. He knows it's dark. He knows the wind is against them. He knows they are straining at the oars. He knows that the boat is being battered by the waves. He knows that this has all been going on for hours. So what do you think Jesus is praying?

We know specifically what Jesus prayed on at least one occasion for one of the guys in the boat, His friend, Simon. *"I have prayed for you, Simon, that your faith may not fail"* (Luke 22:32 NIV).

Is that what Jesus was praying for the boys in the boat—that their faith would carry them through the storm safely to the other side? Did He just want them to understand that the secret to getting safely to the other side was not in how well they could sail or how well they could row, but in how well they could believe? Is that what Jesus is praying for you right now?

DAY 9

On the basis of everything they knew and could do, the boys in the boat were going nowhere. Do you ever feel that way about your life? You're doing everything you know to do. You're straining for all you're worth. But it's like everything's against you. Maybe you need to be reminded of the real secret to getting to the other side. *"'Not by might nor by power, but by My Spirit,' says the LORD"* (Zechariah 4:6).

I wonder if that was what Jesus was praying for the boys in the boat. "Come on, guys. You're not going to get through the storm and the struggle by what you know and what you can do. It's who I AM and what I can do for you when you trust in Me." I wonder if that's what Jesus is praying for you right now.

I know another time we're allowed to listen in as Jesus prays for our benefit: *"Father...for the benefit of the people...that they may believe!"* (John 11:42 NIV).

Our greatest benefit is our belief in Jesus—who He is and what He longs to do for us. Why does Jesus wait until the fourth watch of the night? He's trying to get our belief big enough for a breakthrough.

There's one more prayer that Jesus taught us to pray because, when we pray it, we're praying in agreement with His prayers for us. You know this prayer: *"Deliver us from evil"* (Matthew 6:13 NIV).

Maybe you say, "The boys in the boat were just in a nasty storm. Storms are not evil."

But there are evil storms. Saeed Abedini was stuck in one for 3.5 years. Praise God, Jesus showed up in the fourth watch of the night, and Saeed and three other Americans were released from an Iranian prison. Saeed, an American pastor, was in Iran with that government's permission to build an orphanage. While

"I AM" CRAZY

there, Saeed was arrested for being a Christian. For 3.5 years, he suffered beatings and torture while his wife, his children, and his church here in the States prayed and agonized for his release. My wife, Deb, and I and millions of other believers prayed for Saeed's release for years. On January 16, 2016, during the fourth watch of the night, Jesus set Saeed free.

Whatever storm has come against your life, know that Jesus is praying for you. In fact, let me give you one more glimpse into the prayer life of Jesus. This is what He prays for us: *"Father, I want those You gave Me to be with Me, right where I am. So they can see My glory..."* (John 17:24 NIV).

The heart of Jesus is for us to experience His glory. Passionately, He prays for us to align our lives with His—to think what He thinks, to feel what He feels, to join Him in His work. He watches and waits as we strain in the storms of life. He's been there before us. He's ready to miraculously come to us in whatever way is best to get our belief big enough for a break-through.

Wherever you need a break-through in your life right now, join Jesus in His prayers for your faith to bring about your deliverance and your experience of His glory in your life.

Today's Crazy Big Idea: Jesus is praying for our faith to get big enough for a breakthrough in our stormy struggles.

Today's Crazy Scripture: *"Father, I want those You gave Me to be with Me, right where I am, so they can see My glory!"* (John 17:24 NIV).

Today's Crazy Prayer Starter: "Dear Lord, as I find myself in a stormy struggle, it's good to know You are praying for me and watching over me even when I cannot see You or a way through. Help me build my belief big enough for You to do a breakthrough. Come and deliver me. For Your sake, Amen."

"I AM" CRAZY

"I AM" CRAZY
DAY 10

I was terrified, and I wasn't handling it well. I was sitting alone in the dark in our kitchen at home. My wife was still in Haiti. She had been living there for nine of the last eleven months. It was getting to me—microwave dinners, piles of adoption paperwork, empty bank account, government roadblocks at every turn.

For over a year, we had been trying to adopt a young boy in Haiti. We did everything we were supposed to do. We thought we were doing what God had called us to do. But I was scared to death that it would never work out. My deepest fear was the humiliation of failure. I was afraid that, once again, my best efforts would not be good enough. I was terrified that no one would ever believe in me again.

Now, as I write this, I know it's not about people believing in me but believing in God. However, at that time, my mind was a mess.

I felt like screaming. So I did—at God. I really let Him have it. I shouted at the ceiling, "What is the benefit of knowing You?" Those were my exact words. But I wasn't done.

"What is the benefit of serving You if You don't come through when I need you?"

After a few moments, I got a grip on my emotions. I apologized to the Lord and opened my Bible. It had become my "life preserver" through that stormy struggle. You won't believe the text I was led to read. True story—I'm not making this up—Psalm 103:1-5.

"*Praise the LORD, O my soul, all my inmost being, praise His holy name. Praise the LORD, O my soul, and forget not all His benefits!*" Now He had my full attention.

"*Who forgives all your sins and heals all your diseases; who redeems your life from the pit and crowns you with love and compassion; who satisfies your desires with good things...*" BINGO!

I began to pray Psalm 103 to the Lord. I began to worship Him for His great goodness. I began to remind the Lord that the good thing I desired was for Wilky to be my son.

One month later, the boy Jesus had put on my heart, He put in my home. Praise God!

That's how Jesus came to me in my dark night of stormy struggle. Here's how he came to the boys in the boat.

"*They saw Jesus approaching the boat, walking on the water, and they were terrified. But He said to them, 'It is I; don't be afraid!'*" (John 6:19, 20 NIV).

That's how we read it and hear it in English. But that's not what Jesus actually said, and it is definitely not what His disciples heard. To show you how profoundly dramatic this was, I have to show it you the way Jesus literally declared it, as it appears in Greek.

"*Egw eimi (I AM); mai phobeisthe (fear not)!*"

While they've still got a death-grip on the side of the bobbing, bouncing boat, they hear Jesus declare Himself to be I AM, Yahweh, the God who causes to be. He backed up His claim by supernaturally overcoming all natural laws by walking on water.

There's nothing in all creation that can stop Jesus from getting to us when we're being battered by a stormy struggle. He is greater that any earthly difficulty we face because Jesus is the Lord of all creation. *"We look at this Son (Jesus) and see God's original purpose in everything created. For everything, absolutely everything, above and below, visible and invisible, rank after rank after rank of angels—everything got started in Him and finds its purpose in Him. He was there before any of it came into existence and He holds it together right up to this moment"* (Colossians 1:16,17 MSG).

Just to show you how creative Jesus can be when He comes to us in our stormy struggle, check out the intriguing detail Mark adds to the story: *"Then He climbed into the boat with them, and the wind died down"* (Mark 6:51).

I love the fact that the storm still rages until Jesus gets into the boat with His men. The closer we are with the great "I AM," the less effect the storm has on us.

I'm also surprised that this Lord of Creation, who supernaturally walks on water, decides to humanly climb into the boat. Why didn't Jesus do a Jedi move from above the water to hovering over the side of the boat? Or why didn't Jesus do a ninja move and launch Himself into a double front flip, hitting a perfect landing in the boat? Or why didn't Jesus do a slick Steph Curry move—behind His back, between His legs, a step back, then shoot into the boat from beyond 3-point range? (Sorry, I'm writing this during the N.B.A. Finals). Seriously, why did Jesus physically climb into the boat?

Maybe He wants to settle down the disciples, who have come a bit unglued after riding out a violent storm. One thing for sure, Jesus never did a miracle just to show off. Everything He did was meant to teach a lesson. Maybe the lesson here is that Jesus is fully, walking-on-water God and at the same time, a fully, climbing-into-the-boat man.

This way, they would know later when Jesus agonized through His crucifixion that He suffered every twinge and torment of horrific pain in paying for their sins. He took upon Himself the unholy terror of hell's fury, so they would never have to be terrified again.

His disciples certainly grasped the unmistakable reality that Jesus was and is fully God. *"Those who were in the boat worshipped Him, saying: 'Truly, You are the Son of God!'"* (Matthew 14:33 NIV).

The worship in the boat was prelude to another miracle of Jesus with the boat. As your faith breaks out in worship, you set the stage for Jesus to work more wonders in your life. *"Immediately the boat reached the shore where they were heading!"* (John 6:21 NIV).

Jesus can get you through any storm and, at the same time, satisfy your desires with good things. Praise the Lord, and forget not all his benefits.

DAY 10

Today's Crazy Big Idea: Nothing in all creation can stop Jesus from getting to us when we're being battered by a stormy struggle.

Today's Crazy Scripture: *"I AM!" Fear not!"* (John 6:20 NIV).

Today's Crazy Prayer Starter: "Praise the Lord, O my soul, all my inmost being, praise His holy name! Praise the LORD, O my soul, and forget not all His benefits—who forgives all your sins and heals all your diseases, who redeems your life from the pit and crowns you with love and compassion, who satisfies your desires with good things."

"I AM" CRAZY

"I AM" CRAZY
DAY 11

Over the course of the past ten days, Jesus has been making His best effort to speak to you. It's His passion to reveal Himself to you. He wants to introduce Himself or re-introduce Himself to you. Jesus longs to re-present Himself to you for who He truly is.

This is huge because it seems like everyone has their opinion on Jesus, like He's a specimen to be examined instead of a personal Savior to be known and worshipped. Everyone makes their own judgments of Jesus. Who's right? Is it possible that lots of people are wrong? What if Jesus is way bigger than our small-minded judgments? What if Jesus is the God who actually wants to be intimately known? What if Jesus is willing to become to you more than just your opinion of Him?

Have you ever had anyone make an unfair judgment about you? They don't really know you, but they've heard some gossip at work, at school, or on Facebook. They have never taken the time to sit down and talk with you, but they have been willing to listen and to talk about you behind your back. They don't know you, but they judge you.

Here's another big question. Have you ever had someone who judges you, but still they want to use you? It's not like they respect you, but they want something from you.

That's exactly the situation in which Jesus finds Himself in our text today. Let me set the stage for you. Thirteen men climb out of a boat. Jesus is one of them. Twelve of them are soaking wet. They've been on a wild, night-long boat ride. Intriguingly, Jesus Himself is dry as a bone because He had been walking on top of the water.

Waiting on shore to get to Jesus and His twelve disciples is a large crowd. What I don't like about this crowd is that they are a "me-first," manipulative mob. Here's what I like about this crowd. *"They...went...in search of Jesus!"* (John 6:24 NIV).

This is what I like about you. You are reading this book in search of Jesus. You may not even yet believe that Jesus is the Son of the living God. But you are searching. That shows you are open-minded. That means you're willing to investigate the truth. That means, I believe, you will find Jesus. That's what happens next in our text.

"When they found Him..." (John 6:25 NIV). This is something I love about Jesus. He makes Himself available. He keeps Himself accessible. Jesus wants to be found.

When you seriously, sincerely seek Him, Jesus always is ready to reveal who He is to you and what He wants to do for you.

Consider how Eugene Peterson speaks to this in his Message version of the Bible: *"When you come looking for Me, you'll find Me. When you get serious about finding Me and want it more than anything else, I'll make sure you won't be disappointed! I'll turn things around for you!"* (Jeremiah 29:13,14 MSG).

DAY 11

This is the Jesus I've found. He's a "turn-around" Jesus. He will turn around a marriage that's in trouble. He will turn around children that are in trouble. He will turn around financial trouble. He will turn your soul around from hell and give you a place in heaven.

You name the trouble, and Jesus will turn it to triumph if you seek Him with all your heart.

Unfortunately, this crowd waiting for Jesus was not a welcome party. They were not seeking with all their heart. They were only interested in using Jesus to get what they wanted. I've been guilty of that. Have you ever done that? Your prayers are more like ordering Jesus around, "Jesus, do this. Jesus, do that." If He doesn't do what you tell Him, you get mad at Him. It's like you're God, and He's your servant.

Check out how this crowd was trying to suck up to the Savior, just to get what they wanted. *"When they found Him ...they asked Him, 'Rabbi (Teacher), when did You get here?'"* (John 6:25 NIV). "How are you doing, Jesus? You're looking really good."

These guys are trying to schmooz Jesus with a little chit chat. This is one of those situations where you have to watch the guy patting you on the back because he may be looking for a place to stick the knife.

Jesus is not fooled by the smoke screen. He sees right into their hearts. *"Jesus answered, 'I tell you the truth, you are looking for Me not because you saw the miraculous signs, but because you ate the loaves and had your fill!'"* (John 6:26 NIV).

To get what Jesus is saying to these guys, you have to understand what Jesus did less than 24 hours earlier. The day before—all day long—Jesus had been teaching a throng of thousands. For hours, they had hung on every word. At day's end, they were hungry.

If you are unfamiliar with this account, Jesus takes a little boy's lunch, holds it up before God the Father, thanks His Heavenly Father for it, and calls down God's goodness on it.

Then Jesus multiplies and distributes it to His disciples, who distribute and multiply it to people in the audience, who distribute and multiply it as they share with each other until everyone has enough to eat and more. In fact, there are 12 basketfuls of leftovers.

Now here's the all-important point of Jesus feeding and completely satisfying all those thousands of people. Jesus did not work this miracle just to feed empty bellies. What Jesus did was first and foremost meant to be a miraculous sign.

A sign is used to point to something. Jesus uses the miraculous sign of feeding the five thousand to point to Himself—that He is God. Who other than God could do such a wondrous work? The miracle was an almighty authentication that everything Jesus had taught throughout the day was the Word of God. The meal Jesus fed them would only last a matter of hours. But the Word of God Jesus taught them would be a sustaining strength over any struggle for an entire life-time.

The Word of God is Jesus' primary method of revealing Himself to us. He is not trying to shape our opinion of Him. He's trying to shape our relationship with Him. People who only have opinions about us simply do not have a relationship with us.

We must earnestly seek Jesus; it's not for what we want but for what He wants to give. For sure, He always gives us signs in His Word that point out to us that He is God.

DAY 11

Today's Crazy Big Idea: God's Word is Jesus' primary way of revealing Himself to us.

Today's Crazy Scripture: *"Let the peace of Christ rule in your hearts...Let the Word of Christ dwell in you richly..."* (Colossians 1:15,16 NIV).

Today's Crazy Prayer Starter: "Dear Lord, please point me to who you are. I am so grateful that You are a 'turn-around' Jesus. As I open myself to Your Word, turn around anything in my life that's drifting away from You. I want more than an opinion of You. I want a real relationship with You. In Your name, Amen!"

"I AM" CRAZY

"I AM" CRAZY
DAY 12

Think of the times in your life when someone used you. It's not like they wanted to truly be your friend. They just wanted what you could get or do for them. So they used you. As soon as they got what they wanted, they didn't think twice about dropping you out of their life. It felt like you didn't matter at all. You were just a means to an end.

I wonder if Jesus ever gets tired of people just wanting to use Him. Some want Him to be their "lucky rabbit's foot" Jesus—small enough to carry around in their pocket, so everything goes well with their life. If stuff starts going wrong, just toss this Jesus away. Some want a "genie in a lamp" Jesus. When they need Him, they rub three times and say a little prayer. Jesus is supposed to pop out and grant their wish. When they're done with Jesus, He easily goes back in the lamp. Of course, there's lottery-ticket Jesus. For a small gamble, these folks look for a big payday from their $3 Jesus.

In our text today, a "me-first" mob wants what they can get from the Lord. Jesus doesn't hesitate to lay it out straight. He isn't a "vending machine" Jesus—simply cross your fingers, say a prayer, pull a lever, and get whatever you want. No, Jesus is God.

"I AM" CRAZY

I love the way Eugene Peterson handles what Jesus says to this crowd that just wants to use Him: *"'You've come looking for Me not because you saw God in My actions but because I fed you, filled your stomachs and for free!'"* (John 6:26 MSG).

Before I go on, I want us to get the big picture here. Jesus will continue to address this crowd, but His words are meant as much for His own disciples. Everyone in this picture is Jewish—the crowd, Jesus, and His disciples. All of them have been born and raised in the Jewish faith. The crowd is suspicious of Jesus. They just want Jesus for what He can do for them. The disciples adore Jesus. They will do whatever they can for Him. Jesus is trying to reveal Himself as God's one and only Son to both these groups at the same time with the same teaching. Now we're in the mix as well. We're eavesdropping on this teaching. We're not Jewish, but we're witnesses to this revealing.

With that in mind, we're ready for what happens next. Speaking to the crowd, His disciples and to us, Jesus says: *"'Do not work for food that spoils, but for food that endures to eternal life, which the Son of Man will give to you. For on Him God the Father has placed His seal of approval!'"* (John 6:27 NIV). Jesus is talking our language. He's saying, "Everyone's a consumer. But you get to choose what you consume."

Jesus says, "You can waste your life consuming stuff that doesn't matter—money, cars, houses, clothes, TV's. You can waste your life on some things that won't last. Or you can invest your life in Someone who is forever and offers you life forever." Jesus says, "There is a spiritual food you can consume that will give you abundant, eternal life."

There's only one place you can get it. Jesus is happy to give it to you.

Notice the sharp contrast: you have to work your head off for the things that spoil. Eternal life is a gift that Jesus freely gives. *"I came so they can have real and eternal life, more and better life than they ever dreamed of"* (John 10:10 MSG).

How do we know that Jesus can deliver on this kind of promise? Here's how. He bears the seal of God's approval. In the day of Jesus, a seal was synonymous with authority.

I love the way the Apostle Paul describes how Jesus bears the authority to deliver on all the promises of God. *"He (Christ) is before all things and in Him all things hold together. He is the Head …that in everything He might have the supremacy. For God was pleased to have all His fullness dwell in Him (Jesus)!"* (Colossians 1:17-19 NIV).

Jesus is appealing to this crowd and to His disciples and to us that they—that we—might believe that He is God's one and only Son, sent by God, and sealed by God.

The crowd is not buying what Jesus is declaring about Himself. In fact, they throw the focus back on themselves. *"They asked Him, 'What must we do to do the works God requires?'"* (John 6:28 NIV). How do we get on God's good side?

Jesus is like, "Dude, every side of God is good!" *"Jesus answered, 'The work of God is this: to believe in the One He sent!'"* (John 6:29 NIV).

You don't have to be so holy. You don't have to do so many good deeds. In fact, the only thing that needs doing was done when Jesus died for our sins. Jesus did His part when He took our place on the cross and gave Himself up to the death we should have died. Jesus did His part as our substitute. He took the punishment we deserved. Jesus did His part when He took on Himself all God's anger due us, all God's judgment due us, all of God's condemnation due us for our sin. When He went to hell so we could go to heaven, Jesus did His part.

God the Father did His part when He raised Jesus from the dead; when He exalted Jesus to the highest place. When He gave Jesus the name above all names, God the Father did His part.

Our part is to believe that Jesus is God—come to earth through human birth—fully God, fully man. Our part is to believe that Jesus flawlessly battled His way over every temptation until He had lived a sinless life—He knew no sin and did no sin. Our part is to believe that Jesus willingly laid that utterly innocent life down on the cross to pay for our sin. Our part is to believe that God raised Jesus from the dead. That's our part.

This is our promise: *"If you confess with your lips that Jesus is Lord and believe in your heart that God raised Him from the dead you will be saved"* (Romans 10:9 NIV).

Jesus refuses to be used, but He is utterly willing to be experienced. *"This is how we come to understand and experience love: Christ sacrificed His life for us"* (I John 3:16 MSG).

Today's Crazy Big Idea: Jesus refuses to be used, but He is utterly willing to be experienced!

Today's Crazy Scripture: *"This is how we come to understand and experience love: Christ sacrificed His life for us"* (I John 3:16 MSG).

Today's Crazy Prayer Starter: Dear Jesus, thank You for doing Your part on the cross as my substitute. Thank you for taking my punishment to pay for my sins. Thank You, Heavenly Father, for doing Your part—raising Jesus from the dead and exalting Him to the highest place. Holy Spirit, please help me do my part by believing in the flawless, finished work of Jesus and trusting Him for more and better life. In His name, Amen.

"I AM" CRAZY

"I AM" CRAZY
DAY 13

"No matter how many promises God has made, they are 'Yes' in Christ" (II Corinthians 1:20 NIV).

Which do you think is the best way to be on the receiving end of the miraculous—trying to manipulate the LORD or making much of Jesus?

Let's observe Jesus as He faces a mob that kicks into manipulation mode. *"They asked Him, 'What miraculous sign then will You give that we may see it and believe You? What will You do?'"* (John 6:30 NIV).

Have you ever been this way with Jesus? "Jesus, give me a miracle, and I'll believe in You. Don't give me what I ask, and I'm done with You."

Here's what was driving the manipulative mob. *"Our forefathers ate the manna in the desert; as it is written: 'He gave them bread from heaven to eat!'"* (John 6:31 NIV).

Everybody in this audience knew what these guys were talking about. This was a hugely famous part of their national history. They were talking about a phenomenal, unprecedented miracle performed by God in behalf of His people.

"I AM" CRAZY

If you are not Jewish, you may not be familiar with this story. So let me tell you what happened. God had used Moses to rescue His people out of slavery in Egypt. They were traveling en masse through a desert region to get to the Mountain of God. They were on their way to the same place where Moses had encountered the LORD in a burning thorn bush; to the precise location where God first declared His name. *"I am I AM...This is My name forever, the name by which I am to be remembered from generation to generation"* (Exodus 3:14,15 NIV).

This is extraordinary. This is exactly what God promised Moses at the burning bush when He said, *"I will be with you. And this will be the sign to you that it is I who have sent you. When you have brought the people out of Egypt, you will worship God on this mountain"* (Exodus 3:12 NIV).

Consider what a colossal, mind-blowing miracle this was. Moses had to go up against the greatest military power of that day. He had to gain the release of every Israeli from slavery in Egypt. Then he had to herd hundreds of thousands of them through a barren desert to the mountain of God.

This illustrates the truth of Jeremiah 32:17: *"Ah, Sovereign LORD, You have made the heavens and the earth by Your great power and outstretched arm. Nothing is too hard for You!"* Indeed, this is a great God, worthy of all adoration.

However, the Israelites were more prone to whining than they were to worship. Have you ever been on a trip with your family? And from the backseat, you hear whining cries, "We're hungry. We don't have anything to eat. Why didn't we stay home?"

That's the kind of whining and whimpering Moses was getting from God's people, except there were about a million of

DAY 13

them. Here's what happened: *"Then the LORD says to Moses, 'I will rain down bread from heaven for you'"* (Exodus 16:4 NIV).

Notice the utter generosity of God. He rains down His blessing. He doesn't just sprinkle a little here and there. God rains down His abundant goodness.

This *"bread from heaven"* was called manna. Do you know what "manna" means? It means, "What is this?" The Israelites crawled out of their tents, saw the bread from heaven, and said, "Manna! (What is this?)" It came to mean, "Who did this?"

When God gave His people manna, He wanted them to eat the "Who," so they would worship "Who" gave it to them. But the "Who" meant more. The manna was meant to point to the coming of Jesus, who would be the "Yes" to every promise of God.

Jesus makes a pointed comparison between Himself and manna. *"It is My Father, who gives you the True Bread from heaven. For the Bread of God is He who comes down from heaven and gives life to the world"* (John 6:32,33 NIV).

Here's how manna is meant to make us remember Jesus. Manna was small (Exodus 16:14), pointing to the humility of Jesus, who *"made Himself nothing"* (Philippians 2:7). Manna was round (Exodus 16:14) with no beginning and no end, indicating the everlasting nature of Jesus (Hebrews 7:3). Manna was white (Exodus 16:31), identifying with the purity of Christ, *"a lamb without blemish or defect"* (I Peter 1:19). Manna was sweet (Exodus 16:31), pointing to the absolute goodness of Jesus (Acts 10:38). Manna was nourishing (Psalm 78:25), identifying Jesus as our sustaining strength (Hebrews 1:3).

Just like manna (Exodus 16:4), Jesus came down from heaven (John 6:32,33). Manna was given for a rebellious people (Exodus 16:3) just as Jesus came to seek and to save the lost (Luke 19:10). Manna came down right to where God's people were (Exodus 16:13,14) just as Jesus *"became flesh and dwelt among us"* (John 1:14). With manna being found on the ground (Exodus 16:14), they had to kneel down to receive it. In the same way, every knee will bow before Jesus (Philippians 2:10).

Finally and most importantly to me is the grace connection between manna. Moses said to God's people, *"In the morning you will see the glory of God, because He has heard your grumbling against Him"* (Exodus 16:7 NIV). Instead of being punished for their grumbling, they received a good gift from God. That's grace. And that's our glorious experience through a real relationship with Jesus. *"How much more will those who received God's abundant provision of grace and the gift of righteousness reign in life through the one Man, Jesus Christ!"* (Romans 5:17 NIV).

So capping off His teaching to His Jewish audience then and to us now, Jesus makes it clear that the most important miracle anyone can ever experience is an all-consuming relationship with Him. **"Then Jesus declared, 'I AM the Bread of Life!'"** (John 6:35 NIV).

DAY 13

Today's Crazy Big Idea: Jesus Himself is the best miracle anyone can ever experience!

Today's Crazy Scripture: *"For no matter how many promises God has made, they are all 'Yes' in Christ!"* (II Corinthians 1:20 NIV).

Today's Crazy Prayer Starter: "Heavenly Father, please forgive me for all the time I waste griping and groaning. You have been nothing but good to me every day of my life. I am grateful You do not *"treat us as our sins deserve or repay us according to our iniquities,"* but *"as far as the east is from the west, so far have You removed our sins from us."* Most of all, I thank you for Jesus, my Bread of Life. In His name, Amen."

"I AM" CRAZY

"I AM" CRAZY

DAY 14

I am absolutely convinced that Jesus longs to reveal Himself to you—reveal Himself in your heart, in your home, and in all that happens in your life. Jesus longs to give you a deeply personal and profound experience of His love.

For me, one of my most profound experiences of God's love did not happen at church. It actually happened in our bathroom at home. Please, no wise cracks about having a moving experience in the bathroom. At the time, it was not funny to me at all. This was about 30 years ago. I'd been married for 12 years. I'd been the pastor here for 5 years. I had an 8 year old son and a 5 year old son. But I did not want to leave that bathroom.

I sat on the edge of the tub with my face in my hands, crying out to God. We were not having marital problems or financial problems. The problem was me. I had this deep inner ache. I wanted to be fully loved by someone who knew me inside and out—all my weaknesses, all my flaws. I wanted someone who knew everything about me, to love me and fill the empty, gaping hole in my heart. What was the matter with me?

The longer I sat on the edge of the tub, the more my head and heart dropped. I knew it was absolutely unrealistic to expect my wife or boys to love me the way I wanted to be loved; but if not my own family, then who? When I got to the bottom of myself, I knew Who. In the utter quiet of our bathroom, I sensed the presence of God sighing, "Know Me; know love!"

Do you know what else I sensed in that moment? I sensed my own sin. That was my problem, being too self-focused. When I should have been thinking about God, I was thinking about myself. It's a sad little world that is shrunk down to self-absorption.

So when I walked out of the bathroom that day, I did so with a new perspective. I was determined to shape my life around knowing God more fully; knowing God more deeply.

Here's what I believe: **Know God; Know Love! Know God More Fully, Know Love More Fully! Know God More Deeply, Know Love More Deeply! No God, No Love!**

As a result, there is a scrap of Scripture I've been praying every day for myself and that I've been praying every day for whoever reads this book. *"I ask the God of our Master, Jesus Christ, the God of glory—to make you intelligent and discerning in knowing Him personally!"* (Ephesians 1:17 NIV).

So if you've been feeling extra intelligent lately, that's because I've been praying for you. Actually, this is way bigger and way better and way more important than extra intelligence. This is all about an extra experience of the Lord's profound love for you.

So each day, *"I pray that you ...grasp how wide and how long and how high and how deep is the love of Christ, and that you know*

DAY 14

this love that surpasses all knowledge—that you may be filled to the full with the fullness of God!" (Ephesians 3:18,19 NIV).

One of the ways you come to know and experience the Lord is by knowing His name. That's what Moses found out. Moses was simply minding his own business one day, trying to get His sheep to pasture when God draws him to Himself, just as God is trying to draw you to Himself right in this moment.

When it happened to Moses, God gave him a mission impossible kind of assignment —rescue the nation of Israel from slavery in Egypt. Moses wanted a bit of clarification. *"Moses said to God, 'Suppose I go to the Israelites and say to them, "The God of your fathers has sent me to you," and they ask me, "What is His name?" Then what shall I tell them?' God said to Moses, 'I am ...I AM!...This is My name forever, the name by which I am to be remembered...'"* (Exodus 3:13-15).

This is how God is to be known forever—by His name—**"I AM!"** So when Jesus goes public with His mission and the message of who He truly is, time after time after time, He reveals Himself as the great "I AM!"—"I AM the Bread of Life"; "I AM the Door"; "I AM the Way, the Truth and the Life"; "I AM the Good Shepherd"; "I AM the Resurrection and the Life"! Every single time, it was an open, definitive declaration that Jesus is God—as much God as God the Father is God. Jesus is the Son of the Living God.

The God-encounter with Moses was 1400 years before Jesus came to earth as a baby at the first Christmas. Remember, Jesus spoke to Moses from the fiery glow of a burning thorn bush. In today's story, Jesus declares Himself as the great "I AM" in the brilliant, blazing glow of another fire ceremony—a huge, huge, huge fire ceremony.

"I AM" CRAZY

Moses was all alone out in the desert when he meets the great "I AM!" In today's story, Jesus makes His stunning "I AM" declaration in the most public and dramatic way possible. He does it right in the middle of a major holiday celebration in the big, bustling city of Jerusalem. He does it in the holiest of Jewish places—the Temple of God.

Now here's what you have to imagine. It's night and very dark—"no electricity" dark. It's like waiting for the fireworks on the 4th of July. Do you know the feeling a child gets—the anticipation of waiting and waiting as the night gets darker and darker so the fireworks can begin? That's what's going on in the Temple in Jerusalem on this special holiday evening. Thousands of people are jammed into the worship area, breathlessly waiting for the light show to begin. The air is electric with expectancy. There will be music, singing, and dancing once the light show begins.

There are four colossal candelabras, positioned, one along each wall of the temple court. These candelabras are 80 feet tall. There are four big branches on each candelabra and the top of each branch contains 2.5 gallons of oil. Boom, boom, boom, —the night comes alive with blazing, fiery brilliance when the 16 branches are ignited.

The point of this breath-taking light show was to celebrate the fact that God had promised to send a great Someone who would be a divine light to defeat all darkness.

"There will be no more gloom for those living in distress...The people walking in darkness have seen a great Light; on those living in the land of the shadow of death a Light has dawned!" (Isaiah 9:1,2 NIV).

This is the moment when Jesus goes public and claims to be God's light. In my mind's eye, here's how I see it. While the people are oohing and aahing, before any music is played or there's any singing or dancing, Jesus catches everyone off guard by taking center stage and abruptly shouting for all to hear: *"I AM the Light of the world! Whoever follows Me will never walk in darkness, but will have the Light of life!"* (John 8:12 NIV).

This would make a great tattoo: **"Know Jesus, No Darkness!"**

- - -

Today's Crazy Big Idea: Know God, know love. Know God more fully, know love more fully. Know God more deeply, know love more deeply. No God, no love.

Today's Crazy Scripture: *"I ask the God of our Master, Jesus, the God of glory—to make you intelligent and discerning in knowing Him personally!"* (Ephesians 1:17 MSG).

Today's Crazy Prayer Starter: "Dear Lord, I want to know You with all that I am. I want You to be the Light of my life. I'm sick of the darkness that too often covers my life. Please help me live moment by moment in the light of Your love. For Your sake, Amen.

"I AM" CRAZY

"I AM" CRAZY
DAY 15

I don't know which was more explosive—the huge candelabras turning the darkness into light or Jesus proclaiming, *"I AM the Light of the world!"* (John 8:12 NIV).

There was a moment of silence as Jesus' declaration echoed in the air. Then the whole night goes nuts. Those who believed Jesus filled the temple with full-throated cheers. *"Even as Jesus spoke, many put their faith in Him!"* (John 8:30 NIV).

But an equal, angry number had one murderous thought: do whatever it takes right now to shut Jesus up. *"At this, they picked up stones to stone Him, but Jesus hid Himself, slipping away from the temple grounds!"* (John 8:59 NIV).

What was it that made all these people go so crazy when Jesus cried out, "I Am the Light of the world"? Jews at that time believed God was synonymous with light. *"The LORD is my Light!"* (Psalm 27:1). *"The LORD will be your everlasting Light!"* (Isaiah 60:19). *"By His Light I walked through darkness!"* (Job 29:3). *"When I sit in darkness, the LORD will be a light to me!"* (Micah 7:8).

These are nice, inspirational scriptures, but in the nitty-gritty of our lives, what difference does it make that Jesus is the

"I AM" CRAZY

Light of the world? This declaration of Jesus is recorded in John 8:12. For me, I best see the light of Jesus in the preceding verses, John 8:1-11.

This is the famous story of the woman caught in adultery. Some early manuscripts don't include it in the original text. But personally, I believe this text belongs in the Bible.

It pulsates with the light of God's grace for those of us who have been lost in darkness.

This story takes place earlier on the same day that Jesus made His claim to be the Light of the world. Jesus is teaching in the very same temple, where the big light ceremony would take place that very night. He is surrounded by all the people in the temple who hang on His every word. Light is flowing from the lips of Jesus into the people's hearts.

That's when darkness charges into the scene in an effort to extinguish the light. Stomping through the crowd of listeners is an angry mob, disrupting Jesus' teaching.

"The teachers of the Law..." (John 8:3). Could it be that these teachers are jealous of Jesus, who has all the people listening and learning from Him?

"The teachers of the Law and the Pharisees brought in a woman caught in adultery. They made her stand before the group!" (John 8:3 NIV).

Here's how I see this scene. These holier-than-thou religious fanatics come dragging a woman, carried along by the tidal wave of their condemnation and contempt. When they get to Jesus, she collapses on the ground, desperately clutching a bed sheet—the only thing she could gather around her when they violently yanked her out of bed. They get her back on her feet and force her to stand before Jesus and the crowd.

This is how darkness acts. These men feel nothing for this woman. They treat her like she's nothing. **Darkness dehumanizes hurting people!**

When I say things that hurt people, it is evidence of the darkness in me. When you do things that hurt people, it is evidence of the darkness in you.

These religious freaks were just using this woman to get what they wanted. To them, she was just a pawn to be wasted in their game against Jesus. When we use other people to get what we want, it's evidence of the darkness in us. It's evidence of our deep need for Jesus to shine the light of His love into our dark hearts.

Here's the other deal about darkness: **Darkness accuses!**

"They said to Jesus, 'Teacher, this woman was caught in the act of adultery!'" (John 8:4 NIV).

Here's what I want to know: where's the man? Only the woman is being accused.

The darkness of their accusation puts these religious leaders in dangerous, spiritual territory. When we accuse others, it puts us in dangerous, spiritual territory because Satan, the king of darkness, is the ultimate accuser.

In the book of Revelation Satan is called *"The accuser of our brothers and sisters, who accuses them before our God day and night..."* (Revelation 12:10 NIV).

When we accuse others, we're just joining Satan in his dark and deadly work.

But there's a deeper level of darkness that goes beyond accusation. **Darkness makes harsh judgments!**

As more darkness takes over our hearts, accusation is not enough. We decide to level harsh judgment. The ugliness we see in these religious men is what darkness does in us when we judge others. It's what darkness does to us when others judge us.

I am this woman. You are this woman. She's guilty. We're guilty. She did the wrong thing. We've done the wrong thing. It is painful to be judged. We hurt ourselves when we go over to the dark side and judge others. The worst kind of darkness damages our hearts when we harshly judge ourselves. Self-condemnation kills the soul.

It's a good thing that Jesus, the Light of the world, is our good Shepherd, who restores our soul (Psalm 23:3 NIV).

It should not surprise us that the first words spoken by God in the Bible are these: *"'Let there be light' and there was light. God saw that the light was good, and He separated the light from the darkness"* (Genesis 1:3,4 NIV). God has been trying to separate light and darkness in human hearts ever since.

As the Light of the world, Jesus is our only hope of life free of darkness. *"If we walk in the light as He is in the light …the blood of Jesus purifies us from all sin!"* (I John 1:7 NIV).

Today's Crazy Big Idea: Jesus is our only hope of life free of darkness!

Today's Crazy Big Scripture: *"Declare the praises of Him who called you out of darkness into His wonderful light!"* (I Peter 2:9 NIV).

Today's Crazy Prayer Starter: "Dear Lord, thank You for exemplifying what it means to be loving, accepting, merciful, compassionate, and forgiving. I could go on and on. You are full of grace and truth. I'm sorry for accusing others when I should be accepting responsibility for my own sins. Please heal me when others judge me harshly. Let me be more like You, ever looking to help people; not hurt them. In your name, Amen.

"I AM" CRAZY

"I AM" CRAZY

DAY 16

I would never want to be where this woman is, standing publicly, wearing not much more than her guilt and shame. She just wishes they would get it over and done. She knows where this is headed. Those surrounding her are only waiting for the word to stone her. She can see it in their sanctimonious sneers. She's seen it before. They drag helpless victims, with their hands bound behind their backs, to the edge of a ledge with a steep drop-off. They force them to kneel. They kick them backwards off the ledge. The stones begin to fly and don't stop their punishment until the victim is dead. She's thinking, "If that's where this is going, let's skip this horrible humiliation and get to your dirty work."

She's been accused and judged. But the worst is yet to come when **darkness condemns!**

The religious leaders spit out the words: *"'In the Law Moses commanded us to stone such women!'"* (John 8:5 NIV).

These men are locked and loaded. They already have a death-grip on stones in their hands. But they want to do more than stone the woman. They are looking as well for some way to condemn Jesus. Condemnation is addictive.

They have their hands on Jesus' back, feeling for a place to stick the knife when they ask Him, *"'Now what do You say?' They were using this question as a trap, in order to have a basis for accusing Him"* (John 8:6 NIV).

Condemning others is like a dark drug. You get a little fix by condemning one person. Then you are right-now ready for another hit as you look for someone else to condemn.

That's darkness. That's what it does in us when we accuse, judge, and condemn. It's what it does to us when we are accused, judged, and condemned.

But here's the best news you'll ever hear: **When you follow Jesus, His light defeats, devastates, and dominates all darkness!**

Remember what Jesus promised: *"Whoever follows Me will never walk in darkness, but will have the Light of life!"* (John 8:12 NIV).

In our story, Jesus shows us exactly how this works. First, **the light of Jesus defeats the darkness with kindness!**

While the religious leaders wait for Jesus to respond, He shines on them the light of His loving kindness. Why would Jesus show these judgmental jerks loving kindness? For the same reason He shows us loving kindness when we are judgmental jerks.

"God's kindness leads you to repentance!" (Romans 2:4 NIV).

We sin like the religious leaders were guilty of sin. We sin like the woman was guilty of sin. When we sin, Jesus doesn't criticize us. He is not cruel to us. When we sin, Jesus uses His kindness to lead us to repentance. To repent means to change your mind.

Here's how Jesus tried to change the minds of the religious men. He kneels down to the ground. He takes His finger and begins to write in the dirt. I believe He's writing the names of each of these men. He does so in love. He wants them to follow Him.

All this time, they keep badgering Jesus. When He's finished writing all of their names, He looks up and says, *"'If anyone of you is without sin, let him be the first to throw a stone at her'"* (John 8:7 NIV).

Then once again, He goes back to using His finger to write in the dirt. I believe, by each name, Jesus writes the specific sin of which that particular man is guilty. Then I think Jesus wipes it all away—wipes away every name and every mention of sin. He does not publicly judge, accuse, and condemn them as they have the woman and as they wanted to do to Him. He shows them the light of His kindness. And it works. The kindness of God defeats the darkness. The men drop their rocks. They don't follow Jesus. They walk away defeated.

Now it's just Jesus and the scantily-clad, deeply relieved, obviously stunned woman. *"Jesus straightened up and asked her, 'Woman, where are they? Has no one condemned you?' 'No one, sir,' she said. 'Then neither do I condemn you.'"* (John 8:10,11 NIV).

The light of Jesus devastates the darkness with mercy. Do you know what mercy is? Mercy is the powerful light of Jesus protecting us from the bad stuff we deserve for the bad stuff we've done.

I believe all hell went ballistic when Jesus showed this woman mercy. I believe the kingdom of darkness is absolutely devastated when we get God's mercy instead of the consequences we deserve. Satan has a melt-down. "No, they are guilty. This is out-right, blatant sin. They deserve to be punished." He lifts his finger of accusation and points out our every sin. But Jesus lifts His hand and points to the scars— irrefutable evidence that He died on the cross and rose from the dead to offer us mercy and protect us from the awful consequences of our sin.

But Jesus is not done—not with the devil, not with the woman, and not with us. To the woman, *"Jesus declared, 'Go now and leave your life of sin!'"* (John 8:11 NIV).

The light of Jesus dominates the darkness with grace! Do you know what grace is? Remember mercy. Mercy is God protecting us from the bad stuff we deserve. Grace is God giving us good gifts we don't deserve. Grace is greater than even our greatest sin.

"In Him was life and that life was the Light...The Light shines in the darkness; the darkness could not put it out!" (John 1:5 NIV, MSG).

DAY 16

Today's Crazy Big Idea: We are great sinners. But the grace of Jesus is greater than even our greatest sin.

Today's Crazy Scripture: *"There is now no condemnation, for those who are in Christ Jesus!"* (Romans 8:1 NIV).

Today's Crazy Prayer Starter: "Dear Lord, how can I ever thank You for Your amazing love? Jesus, on the cross, You took upon Yourself all God's condemnation for my sin. You were my Substitute. You took all my punishment in my place. By Your shed blood, I get loving kindness, mercy, and grace—all from God. For Your sake, Amen."

"I AM" CRAZY

"I AM" CRAZY
DAY 17

Life is a challenge. Life is one challenge after another. If you want to be good at life, you have to be good at challenges. Often life throws multiple challenges at us all at the same time. School is a challenge. Work is a challenge. Together, they can make a double challenge. Marriage is a challenge. Parenting is a challenge. Marriage is even more of a challenge when you stir parenting challenges into the mix. Not to mention the times we must endure health challenges and financial challenges.

Some challenges we don't mind. Other challenges scare us to death. We can handle some challenges all day long. Other challenges are killer. They man-handle us—tear us up. Some challenges seem so difficult, so dogged, so daunting, we want to give up.

What's the greatest challenge or maybe the most painful challenge you're facing right now? Is it a grief challenge or an abuse challenge? Is it a divorce challenge, an addiction challenge, a cancer challenge, or an unemployment challenge?

It felt like the challenges were piling up on me hot and heavy this week. Every week, I face the challenge of preparing a God-inspired, Bible-based, Christ-exalting teaching for our

"I AM" CRAZY

church. Every week, I have the challenge of leading a church that's larger than the town where I grew up. Lately, it feels like my diabetes is a daily physical challenge.

But last Sunday, life went challenge crazy. I'm on the couch that evening just relaxing. Suddenly I'm on the floor, doubled over with terrific pain in my chest. I can hardly move. Breathing is difficult. I feel nauseous and clammy. I try to remember the symptoms of a heart attack, but my brain isn't working well. Deb takes me to the ER. On the way, I tell the Lord I'm ready to go, but I'm concerned about Deby, raising Lovia on her own and getting by financially without me. After several hours at the hospital, I get the diagnosis. It was an attack but not a heart attack. It was acute pancreatitis. I have to go on a liquid diet. What blew my mind is that gravy is not considered a liquid. Come on, man!

Then this week, one of our church members was in a terrible car accident. She's in critical condition. The same night a young woman (37 years old), who's very precious to me and was recently baptized here, passed away unexpectedly. Her parents are some of my closest friends.

By Wednesday morning, I call our staff together for a time of prayer and communion to bring these and other challenging issues before the Lord. After I dismissed the staff, I wrestled with a question through the rest of that day: How did Jesus do this? How did Jesus handle challenges—daily challenges, daunting challenges, pestering challenges, seemingly impossible challenges?

Here's what we know: Jesus faced every challenge we do. "We have…Jesus, the Son of God…One who was in every respect tested (challenged) as we are, yet without committing any sin. So

DAY 17

let's walk right up to Him and get what He is so ready to give. Take the mercy, accept the help!" (Hebrews 4:14-16 MLB, MSG).

Here's what we want to know: How do we get the merciful help of Jesus for the multiple challenges we face in this life? That's the question I have been wrestling with all week. I think we can find the answer by Jesus in a stressful scene where He is confronted by a daunting challenge.

Here's how our text opens today. *"The Pharisees challenged Jesus..."* (John 8:13 NIV).

Pharisees were like the religious mafia of that day. They were extremists—fanatical about religious rules and regulations. They used those rules and regulations to soak money out of people. It was like religious racketeering.

These religious fanatics despised Jesus because He did not abide by their rules. He had little respect for their rules. With Jesus, people were more important than religious rules. Aren't you glad to know that? You and your challenges are more important to Jesus than how good you are. Jesus is all about showing mercy and helping you with your challenges.

These religion Nazis were deeply jealous of Jesus because He was incredibly popular. His popularity was growing all the time. That made them afraid of Jesus. But what made them want to kill Jesus were His repeated declarations that He was equal with God—as much God as God the Father is God. Jesus claimed to be the great "I AM!"

So every chance they got, they were in Jesus' face, challenging Him, disrespecting Him. How much do you hate being disrespected by people who are just jerks? Why did Jesus have to put up with these uncalled for people challenges? If Jesus was God, as He claimed, couldn't He silence His critics? Couldn't

He call down fire from heaven and turn His critics into crispy critters? Why did He have to endure these personal attacks?

Jesus did it for us. He knew we'd suffer people challenges, so He allowed Himself to be a target of attack from mean-spirited, narrow-minded people. Remember Jesus *"...was in every respect tested (challenged) as we are..."*

I like the way Peter reminds us how intimately Jesus identified with the same challenges we face. *"He suffered everything that came His way so you would know that it could be done, and also know how to do it, step by step. He never did one thing wrong, not once said anything amiss. They called Him every name in the book. He said nothing back. He suffered in silence content to let God set things right"* (I Peter 2:21-23 MSG).

Enduring people challenges for us is just another example of how Jesus embraced our unbearable sin challenge. *"Jesus used His servant body to carry our sins to the Cross, so we could be rid of sin, free to live the right way. His wounds became your healing. You were lost sheep with no idea who you were or where you were going. Now you are named and kept for good by the Shepherd of your souls"* (I Peter 2:24,25 MSG).

Whatever challenge you or I are facing right now, Jesus has been there, done that. We've got a great Savior in Jesus from whom, *"we may receive mercy and find grace to help us in our time of need"* (Hebrews 4:16 NIV).

Today's Crazy Big Idea: We can trust Jesus with our challenges. He understands fully.

Today's Crazy Scripture: *"Humble yourselves, therefore under God's mighty hand that He may lift you up in due time. Cast all your (challenges) on Him, because He cares for you"* (I Peter 5:6,7 NIV).

Today's Crazy Prayer Starter: "Dear Lord, thank You for always being there for me. Thank You for always having been in the challenge before me to show me the way. Help me with my people challenges. Help me to be as patient with others as You have been with me. Thank for You for dealing with my sin challenge. In Your name, Amen."

"I AM" CRAZY

"I AM" CRAZY
DAY 18

I've always been a person who loves a challenge. Sometimes, that gets me in trouble.

When I was a lot younger and a lot more foolish, I loved free-style cliff climbing—no ropes; just me and the rock.

I loved it until our family was out in the Rockies one summer on vacation. A friend of mine and I saw a cliff we wanted to climb. He went up first, and I followed. Everything was going well for me until I got near the top. I got myself in a bad position, and I knew it. I had two good footholds and two good places for my hands. I had been a bit overconfident and moved up a bit too fast. I was in a spot where I could not see my next hold. That's when I made a big mistake. I looked down. I just intended to look down to see if I could reposition my feet somehow. But when I looked, my focus went below my feet all the way down to where my young sons were watching on the ground below. A bad thought went through my head. If I fell, it would be really gross. My boys needed a father, not some stupid rock climber. That negative thought turned into paralyzing fear.

Have you ever been in a spot like that where you freeze up with fear? It was like I could not make any kind of move for fear of falling. Finally, I calmed myself down, found a hold above me that I had not seen before. I reached it and made it up that cliff.

There's something I have learned since then that I wish I had known before that climb. It's in a book by Arno Ilgner, *The Rock Warrior's Way!* It's all about how to conquer the fear of falling when climbing.

This is not a Christian book. But let me tell you what I love about the title of this book. First, the Rock—Jesus is our Rock. *"The LORD is my Rock!"* (Psalm 18:2 NIV).

Jesus is a warrior. He's the Commander of the LORD's army. Jesus is the Way. He is the Way through any challenge.

When you're facing a daunting challenge, you can go weak with fear or you can go at it, like a warrior—the Jesus way. If you go at it with fear, you're going down for a hard fall. If you go at your challenge like a warrior, Jesus will help you conquer it.

According to this book, there's a way for every rock climber to overcome fear. A warrior observes. A warrior accepts. A warrior focuses. A warrior intends. A warrior commits.

What I love about this is that these same five steps are exactly the pattern set by Jesus for always being up for whatever challenge or number of challenges life brings your way. Fear makes you fall. **To be a warrior, the secret is certainty!**

Let me show you how Jesus does it. *"The Pharisees challenged Him, 'Here You are, appearing as your own witness; Your testimony is not valid!'"* (John 8:13 NIV).

DAY 18

These religious Nazis are calling Jesus a liar. They are challenging His credibility.

In the *Rock Warrior's Way*, the first step to attacking a challenge is to observe. That's what Jesus does as He faces these religious bad guys who want to see Him dead.

Jesus' observation: Know the certainty of your relationship with your Heavenly Father! This is exactly what you must do when you face a challenge.

Here's how Jesus did it, *"Jesus answered, 'Even if I testify on My own behalf, My testimony is valid, for I know where I came from …'"* (John 8:14 NIV).

Years ago when I was struggling with the challenge of that cliff face, I should have been more observant of the rock. Observation is the first step toward handling the challenge.

The observation that Jesus makes here refers to His relationship with God the Father.

Jesus knew that He had always been with God and had been sent by God. Whatever challenge you're facing right now, the first step toward handling it effectively is to know the certainty of your relationship with the Heavenly Father.

You are a child of the God who works all things together for the good. You are a child of the God who is able to do immeasurably more than all you can ask or imagine. You are a child of the God who is healer. You are a child of the God who is provider. You are a child of El Shaddai, the God who is enough. He's enough for any challenge.

But Jesus is certain of more. He is certain of His destiny. This is what He went on to say: *"My testimony is valid, for I know where I came from and where I am going!"* (John 8:14 NIV).

Jesus knows with certainty He is destined to be exalted to

the right hand of God. Jesus knows with certainty He is to be given the name above all names. Jesus knows with certainty that He is destined to be Lord of lords and King of kings.

In the *Rock Warrior's Way,* the second step to overcoming a challenge is acceptance. **Acceptance: The certainty of your destiny!**

Here's your destiny. *"You can do all things through Christ, who gives you strength"* (Philippians 4:13 NIV). Here's your destiny. *"You are the workmanship of God, created in Christ Jesus, to do great works, which God has prepared in advance for you to do"* (Ephesians 2:10 NIV).

Here's our destiny: *"We are more than conquerors through Him who loved us…neither death nor life, neither angels nor demons, neither the present nor the future, nor any powers, neither height nor depth, nor anything else in all creation, will be able to separate us from the love of God that is in Christ Jesus our Lord!"* (Romans 8:37-39 NIV).

When you are certain that you are going to win in the end, you can face any challenge.

Today's Crazy Big Idea: The secret to conquering every challenge is: certainty of your relationship with your Heavenly Father and certainty of the destiny the Lord has for you!

Today's Crazy Scripture: *"We are more than conquerors through Him who loved us..."* (Romans 8:37 NIV).

Today's Crazy Prayer Starter: "Dear Lord, You're my Rock. You're my way through any challenge. I know You will never leave nor forsake me. You stand by me when life's challenges rise before me. You are my strength and hope. I praise Your name, Amen!"

"I AM" CRAZY

"I AM" CRAZY
DAY 19

In the *Rock Warrior's Way*, the third step to handling any challenge is focus. For us, **our focus must be to avoid the uncertainty of human perspective.**

Jesus tells the religious rule-keepers, *"You judge by human standards..."* (John 8:15 NIV).

Human standards are mere opinions. Everybody has an opinion on everything. Anytime anybody tells you, *"Well, it's my opinion..."* it's an indication they are far from the truth. The truth of God's Word is God's gold standard.

Opinions are temporary. They come and go with whichever way the wind is blowing. Opinions are fake faith. They do not draw deeper into a real relationship with Jesus. In fact, opinions keep us from having a real relationship with Jesus. Having an opinion is like making up your own rules for life. That's what the religious fanatics did. Jesus calls them on it.

Jesus is calling us to anchor our lives to the truth of His Word. Whatever challenge you're facing right now, if you go at it with your opinion or someone else's opinion, you're in for a devastating fall. If you want to overcome any challenge, you have to focus on avoiding human opinion that will not hold up. Anchor your life to the truth that is Jesus. The truth of Jesus is rock-solid, unchanging, and never-failing.

The Rock Warrior's Way goes on to tell us that the next step in overcoming any challenge is **intent—the bigger the challenge, the stronger your intention must be!**

We get our strongest intention: **Praying for the certainty of the Father's perspective!**

Here's how Jesus said it. *"My decisions are right, because I am not alone. I stand with the Father, who sent Me!"* (John 8:16 NIV).

Earlier, I mentioned suffering an attack of acute pancreatitis on a Sunday evening. A normal level of enzymes is considerably lower than 200. Mine shot up well over 200. That caused the severe pain and put me in the ER. When the doctor explained this to me, he said, "Usually someone in your condition is placed in the hospital for five days to a week. You get complete bed rest and are fed through an iv." I said, "How do you get the Big Mac through that little iv tube?" Just kidding. I did tell him that there was no way I could spend 5-7 days in the hospital. I didn't have the time or the money.

I used my Jedi mind tricks on him, and he let me go home with a promise to rest and eat only bland foods. By Thursday, my numbers were over 900. So I went on a strict liquid diet. If things didn't change, I'd have no choice but to go into the hospital for a week.

But two things happened on Friday. First, I unexpectedly bumped into a young mom from our church. She has a daughter, whom I love with all my heart, who's severely disabled.

As we talked, she told me her little girl has acute pancreatitis. Her numbers were in the thousands. My wife was with me, so we put our arms around this mom and called down the goodness of God on her daughter. We prayed for our Heavenly Father to restore normalcy in her pancreas and protect her from any pain or further damage to her body.

After that prayer, Deb and I headed for my office, where we were going to pray and take communion, regarding my pancreatitis. While we're praying, the phone rang. It was an unexpected call from my doctor. She said, "I wanted to get in touch with you as soon as I found out. I studied the results of your blood test from this morning. I can't believe it, but your numbers have gone from over 900 back to normal." I said, "Can I have biscuits and gravy?" She said, "No, but instead of being in the hospital, you will be preaching at your church this weekend!" I dropped a big, "Praise the Lord!" on that doctor (By the way, my little friend's enzyme numbers are back to normal too. God answers prayer!).

That was one of my challenges this week. You have your challenges. The secret to overcoming any challenge or any number of challenges is praying to get the certainty of the Lord's perspective. He is good. He is greater. He offers mercy and hope and help.

In *The Rock Warrior's Way,* the final step to overcome any challenge fearlessly is to commit. Here's what that looked like for Jesus—**commit: know the certainty of your mission in life!**

Jesus clearly establishes who He is and what He's called to do. *"I AM One who testifies for Myself; My other witness is **the Father, who sent Me!**"* (John 8:18 NIV).

Boom! There it is—another "I AM" declaration by Jesus that He is God. He is fully man. He is fully God. And He is fully on mission with His life. His mission was the cross.

"I AM" CRAZY

Twice in John 8, these religious Nazis want to kill Jesus. *"They picked up stones to stone Him, but Jesus hid Himself, slipping away..."* (John 8:59 NIV).

"No one seized Him, because His time had not yet come!" (John 8:20 NIV).

Though it was their full intention, these men were not going to stone Jesus. Jesus would not allow His life to be taken from Him. He alone would decide as He and His Father had planned when, where, and how He would give up His life in sacrifice. He was not going to die in the temple. He was going to die on a cross on a garbage dump. His mission was to die in our place as payment for our sins.

When you are certain of your God-given purpose in life, you can overcome any and all challenges. You have something bigger and better to do with your life, and no challenge is going to stand in the way of you living out God's dream for you.

Do you know your mission in life? Do you know when Jesus received His mission? When He was baptized, Jesus received not only the confirmation of His mission but also the power and presence of God's Holy Spirit to achieve the mission. Then every teaching, every healing, and every miracle was shaped with the certainty of His mission.

What's true for Jesus is true for you. Challenges can't stand up to God's dream for you!

Today's Crazy Big Idea: When you are certain of your God-given purpose in life, you can overcome any challenge.

Today's Crazy Scripture: *"For we are God's handiwork, created in Christ Jesus to do good works, which God prepared in advance for us to do!"* (Ephesians 2:10 NIV).

Today's Crazy Prayer Starter: "Dear Lord, please keep me free of human perspective. Help me anchor my life to Your Truth. You have designed a great destiny for my life. Please fill me with Your Holy Spirit, so I can stay on mission. For your sake, Amen!"

"I AM" CRAZY

"I AM" CRAZY
DAY 20

Our choices are everything! Our lives are shaped by our choices. Whatever your life is right now, it is based on your choices. We cannot control every hard or hurtful thing that comes into our lives, but we never lose our power to choose how we respond to whatever life does. No one gets to choose for us. They can encourage us. They can support us. They can counsel us. They can pray for us. But in the end, it is our responsibility to choose. The choices we make shape our lives.

Typically, people underestimate the power of their choices—either for the good or for the bad. But here's the bottom-line: **Every choice has a ripple effect!** Every good choice ripples out to more good, more good, and more good. Every bad choice has an on-going detrimental and damaging ripple effect.

What is maybe the worst choice you ever made? Was it the choice of a short-term relationship that rippled into long-term pain? Was it a drug or alcohol choice that rippled into addiction? Was it the choice of angry, hurtful words that rippled into a ruined friendship? Was it the choice of clicking onto a website that rippled into pornography?

I learned the negative ripple effect of a bad choice on my first attempt to climb a 14,000 foot peak in the Colorado Rockies. I was with Deby and a group of friends. I had studied the different routes to the top of Mount Princeton. There was an easy route and a hard route. I was young and foolish. I wanted nothing to do with easy. So I led the group up the long, hard route. Once we were above the tree-line, we got caught in a bit of a blizzard when a snow squall stormed over us. We got through that and made it up to a spine of a ridge from which we could make an ascent to the top if we had known what we were doing. I've climbed Mt. Princeton a couple of times since then only to see what a fool I had been that first time.

What I know now that I didn't know then is that we were in a position to make it to the top. We did not make it to the top. We gave up. We were exhausted mentally and physically. I looked down the opposite side of the mountain and said, "That looks like a good way to go down. The way we came is too hard. Let's go that way." Bad choice.

A good choice, if we were not going for the top, would be to go back the way we had come; particularly since people were going to pick us up back at the place where we started. That bad choice to go down the wrong side of the mountain had a very negative ripple effect. The trail I thought was a hiking trail that would take us down soon became only an animal trail—a Rocky Mountain goat trail. We were not Rocky Mountain goats. The goat trail dead-ended at a sheer drop off and a waterfall. We had to climb back above and around that drop off. Even then, my bad choice continued to put us in very dangerous situations. Because God is kind to fools, we made it out safely. Fortunately for me, it became only a live-and-learn life lesson. But here's what I know. Every choice we make for good or for bad has a ripple effect.

Now what's true for you and me in regard to our choices is also true of Jesus with one exception. Jesus does not make any bad choices. Every choice Jesus makes is a profoundly good choice with a phenomenally good ripple effect. Do you know the most incredible choice Jesus makes? **Jesus chooses you!**

What blows my mind is how relentless, stubborn, and doggedly determined Jesus is in His choosing. He chooses you and chooses you and chooses you and chooses you and keeps on choosing you in hopes that you will choose Him back. Jesus never stops choosing you. My whole purpose today is to ask you if you will choose Jesus back.

Let me tell you a story about people making choices. A Jewish rabbi, a Hindu priest, and a politician are driving late at night out in the country when their car breaks down. They walk to a nearby farm house, hoping to spend the night. The farmer graciously welcomes them. But he says, "I only have two extra beds. One of you will have to sleep in the barn." The Jewish rabbi says, "My people wandered in the wilderness. I choose to sleep in the barn." They all go to bed. Ten minutes later, there's a knock at the door. The farmer opens the door. It's the Jewish rabbi who says, "There's a pig in the barn. My faith won't allow me to be around pigs." The Hindu priest says, "I'll sleep in the barn." Everyone goes to bed. Ten minutes later, there is a knock at the door. It's the Hindu priest, who says: "There's a cow in the barn. My faith will not allow me to be around cows." The politician says, "Okay, I'll sleep in the barn." Everyone goes to bed. Ten minutes later, there's a knock at the door. It's the cow and the pig.

"I AM" CRAZY

Right now, our nation is all about choosing a politician to be our president. We choose the candidate that best suits our views. That's how many people go at choosing Jesus. They want to choose Jesus on their own terms. They think, "Jesus is cool." They want a Jesus who makes them feel good about themselves. They think, "I like the idea of a Savior Jesus to forgive my sins. I'd choose a Savior Jesus. A 'bless me' Jesus sounds really good. A 'miracle' Jesus is even better. I'd choose a 'bless me' miracle Jesus. I like the idea of being free of all guilt and shame—I like that. I'd choose a 'comfort me' Jesus. The peace and hope of Jesus—I'd like that. I'd choose a 'help me de-stress' Jesus. Of course, a 'Jesus loves me no matter what' Jesus would be amazing."

Friends, on the Jesus menu, there is only one choice to choose. Jesus chooses you, and He's asking you, pleading with you, appealing to you that you choose Him as Lord.

The good news is once you completely surrender to Jesus as your Lord, then He does forgive your sins; then He does miraculously bless your life; then He does cleanse you of all guilt and shame; then He becomes your comfort, your peace, your hope, your joy. You're able to grasp the height, the depth, the length, and the breadth of His limitless love for you. He fills you to the full with the fullness of God when you choose Jesus to be your Lord. When you choose Jesus as absolute Lord of your life, there's a profound, positive ripple effect as He works everything together for good.

What I find so incredible about Jesus is that He keeps choosing us even when we don't choose Him as Lord. He keeps choosing us even when we get angry with Him for not blessing us; for not giving us a miracle; for not giving us everything we want.

Jesus keeps choosing us, knowing that if we choose to surrender to His Lordship, we will experience overwhelming peace; our hearts will swell with hope and joy; blessings will flow abundantly, and even the miraculous will occur in our unworthy lives.

• •

Today's Crazy Big Idea: Jesus chooses you, and He's pleading with you to choose Him as your Lord.

Today's Crazy Scripture: *"Choose for yourselves this day whom you will serve …as for me and my household, we will serve the LORD!"* (Joshua 24:15 NIV).

Today's Crazy Prayer Starter: "Dear Lord, thank You for choosing me. Thank You for Your passion to keep on choosing me even when I don't deserve it. I am so grateful for your mercy and grace. Please forgive me for my bad choices. Lord, right now I choose to surrender to You. For Your sake, Amen."

• •

"I AM" CRAZY

"I AM" CRAZY
DAY 21

In our story today, Jesus has these holier-than-thou religious types who are attacking Him, accusing Him, condemning Him, disrespecting Him, belittling Him, demeaning Him, hating Him, and wanting to see Him dead. Jesus keeps choosing them and making every effort to move them to choose Him as Lord.

I love the way the account opens with these words: *"Once more Jesus..."* (John 8:21).

Once more, Jesus reaches out to them. Once more, Jesus tries to change their minds about Him. Once more, Jesus loves them. Once more, Jesus offers to be their Lord.

Aren't you glad we have a "once more" Jesus? Aren't you glad that Jesus never gives up on you? You drift away from God. You drift away from church. Jesus keeps coming after you, asking you to choose Him. You do some selfish things. You take your life in a dark direction. Jesus keeps coming after you, extending His hand to you. You ignore His hand. You slap His hand away. Jesus keeps asking you to choose Him as Lord.

I love the fact that I have a "once more" Jesus, who is full of mercy, who loves to show compassion, who is patient, patient,

patient with a jerk like me, who never stops offering me His grace. I am unashamed I choose Jesus as my Lord. Nothing else works.

But before you make the mistake of thinking that Jesus will just let you walk all over Him as He's choosing you, let's see how He gets real with this bunch of really religious people. *"Once more Jesus said to them, 'I am going away and you will look for Me, and you will die in your sin. Where I go, you cannot come!'"* (John 8:21 NIV).

Notice the word "sin" is singular. We all have sins. Jesus is not talking about our many sins. He's talking about one sin in particular. It is the supreme sin—the sin of refusing to choose Jesus as Lord. Jesus makes this clear later in John—*"Their refusal to believe in Me is their basic sin!"* (John 16:9 MSG).

Jesus is not just talking to these religious guys a long time ago. He's speaking to our hearts right now. Jesus makes it clear to one and all for all time. He puts it out there plainly, "I am going to heaven. If you do not believe that I am God; if you do not choose Me to be absolute Lord of your life, you will not go to heaven."

Every choice has a ripple effect. Choosing Jesus as Lord ripples you right into heaven. Refusing to choose Jesus as Lord ripples a person right into hell.

The Jews listening to Jesus will not accept this spiritual reality. They in no way want to admit their need for Jesus in order to go to heaven. *"The Jews said, 'So, is He going to kill Himself? Is that what He means by, "You can't come with Me!"?'"* (John 8:22 MSG).

The Jews believed that suicide was the supreme sin, and the darkest pit in hell was reserved for those who take their own lives. They're saying, *"He must be going to hell, because we know we're going to heaven."*

Jesus keeps reaching out to them; keeps trying to convince them; keeps trying to get them to choose Him as Lord. "Jesus said, *'You are too tied down to the mundane; I am in touch with what is beyond your horizons. You're living in terms of what you can see and touch. I live on other terms'"* (John 8:23 MSG).

What does Jesus mean, *"I live on other terms"*? He means He is God. How do I know? Look at the very next thing Jesus says to the Jews: *"'If you do not believe that I AM, you will indeed die in your sins!'"* (John 8:24 NIV).

"I AM" is God's name. Jesus is declaring Himself to be God—as much God as God the Father is God. Jesus is claiming to be the Son of the living God.

Notice this time Jesus uses the plural form "sins." Here's what He's saying, "If you commit the ultimate sin of refusing to choose Me as Lord, the ripple effect will be dying forever because of your many sins.

But here's the astounding good news. The opposite is also true. If we choose Jesus as our Lord, sin loses its death grip on our souls. All our sins are forgiven—past, present, and future. The choice to make Jesus absolute Lord of your life has a radical ripple effect that will carry you all the way to heaven to be with this Jesus you have chosen.

This marvelous, multi-dimensional truth is perfectly captured in the beauty of John 3:16: *"For God so loved the world that He gave His one and only Son, that whoever believes in Him shall not perish, but have eternal life!"*

It all starts with the **"God-dimension."** Though His heart is broken by your sin, God immediately sets up a saving strategy to offer you a restored relationship with Him. That strategy is the gift of His One and Only Son, Jesus.

This strategy is the **"love-dimension."** *"God put His love on the line for us by offering His Son in sacrificial death, while we were of no use whatever to Him"* (Romans 5:8 MSG).

God's focus is so inclusive, His offer of love is to *"whoever."* Whoever means you. This is the **"you-dimension."** *"It is by grace YOU have been saved!"* (Ephesians 2:8 NIV).

This is all possible by the **"gift-of-Jesus dimension."** Jesus is God's *"indescribable gift"* because *"the blood of Jesus, His Son, purifies us from all sin"* (I John 1:7 NIV).

The word *"believes"* means more than intellectual assent. I call this the **"surrender-dimension."** All the hope of John 3:16 hangs on our willingness to surrender to Jesus.

The word *"perish"* is an eternal perishing. This is the **"hell-dimension."** If we refuse Jesus, we exist forever under the anger and condemnation of God (ie John 3:18,36 NIV).

The phrase *"eternal life"* means *"life as God has it."* This is the **"heaven-dimension."**

It begins for you the moment you surrender to Jesus. It's abundant, joyful, and eternal.

DAY 21

Today's Crazy Big Idea: Our "once more" Jesus never stops choosing us and is always making every effort to get us to choose Him.

Today's Crazy Scripture: *"This is how much God loved the world: He gave His Son, His one and only Son. And this is why: so that no one need be destroyed; by believing in Him, anyone can have whole and lasting Life"* (John 3:16 MSG).

Today's Crazy Prayer Starter: "Dear Father, thank You for the indescribable gift of Jesus. How can I not but surrender to Him as my Savior and Lord? Thank You for Your love that keeps on choosing me; that you never give up on me. I'm grateful that Your grace is greater than my sin. I choose You as My Lord! For Your sake, Amen!"

"I AM" CRAZY

"I AM" CRAZY

DAY 22

Someone's knocking at your front door. You grab the remote; click off the TV. You haul yourself off the couch and head for the door. The knocking continues. You say, "I'm coming. I'm coming." You open the door. Jesus Himself is standing on your front step. He's not wearing a "Hello, My Name Is …" tag. You just know. This is the Son of God. You're dumbfounded. After a moment of stunned silence, you blurt out, "Can I help You?" which makes you feel like a real idiot. Jesus simply smiles and says, "No, but I can help you. I have the greatest news especially for you." You think to yourself, "Oh my gosh, I've won the lottery." Jesus says, "No. It's better than that." Before you can think another thing, the face of Jesus floods with emotion. The love you feel coming from Him about knocks you over. You think He's about to cry, but He never stops smiling and says, *"If you do not believe that I AM, you will indeed die in your sins!"* Jesus gives you one more incredible smile. He then heads over for your neighbors to tell them the very same thing.

It's the very same thing Jesus would say to Billy Graham, to Donald Trump, and Hillary Clinton. It's the same thing Jesus would say to every ISIS terrorist. It's the same thing He

129

would say to every prisoner on death row. It's the same thing He would say to me.

It is what Jesus has wanted to say to every person on the planet since the first time He said it to a bunch of religious haters nearly 2,000 years ago. Jesus loved those holier-than-thou's just like He loves you and Billy Graham and every terrorist and even me.

Jesus may be God. But He's not above begging: *"If you do not believe that I AM, you will indeed die in your sins"* (John 8:24 NIV).

How would you respond to Jesus' pleading? The Jews spat these words at Him: *"Who are You?"* (John 8:25 NIV). This was their way of sneering at Jesus with disgust, *"Who do you think you are?"*

What does it mean to believe that Jesus is God, the great "I AM"? I love the way the Apostle Paul answers that question in Philippians 2:5-9 (MSG): *"Christ Jesus…had equal status with God, but didn't think so much of Himself that He had to cling to the advantages of that status no matter what. Not at all. When the time came, He set aside the privileges of deity and took on the status of a slave, became human. Having become human, He stayed human. It was an incredibly humbling process. He didn't claim special privileges. Instead He lived a selfless, obedient life and then died a selfless obedient death—the worst kind of death at that—a crucifixion. Because of that obedience, God lifted Him high…"*

Here's how Jesus answered the Jews Himself. *"Jesus said, 'When you have lifted up the Son of Man, then you will know that I AM!'"* (John 8:28 NIV).

When Jesus makes this declaration, He lifts up His voice beyond just the really religious rabble-rousers who are in His face. Jesus is convinced that in the larger crowd around Him, there were those who would choose Him when they saw Him on the cross.

I see this happen all the time in the weekend crowds at our church. People see our services climax with others being baptized. Baptism is a picture of the death, burial, and resurrection of Jesus. Baptism is lifting Jesus up in your life. Baptism is the action you take and the experience you have when you choose Jesus to be your Lord.

People see other people, sharing fully in the death, burial, and resurrection of Jesus; having sins forgiven; being cleansed of all guilt and shame; burying their baggage and putting their past behind them. They say, "That's what I want for my life. I want everyone to know that Jesus is my Lord. I want to join Jesus in baptism."

I'm guessing there were people listening to Jesus on this day, who were among the 3,000 baptized on the day the church was born. Here's what we know for sure from our text: *"Even as Jesus spoke, many put their faith in Him!"* (John 8:30 NIV).

These people wanted in them what they saw in Jesus. Something evidently went off in them when they heard Jesus say, *"The One who sent Me is with Me; He has not left Me alone; for I always do what pleases Him!"* (John 8:29 NIV).

They wanted God the Father to always be with them the way He was with Jesus. They wanted to do what would always be pleasing to Him.

So what do you believe if you believe that Jesus is God, the great "I AM"?

First, believe Jesus lives up to His Name. *"His Name is the Word of God!"* (Revelations 19:13 NIV). Believe what John declared: *"In the beginning was the Word, and the Word was with God, and the Word was God!"* (John 1:1 NIV). Believe Paul got it right when he wrote, *"Christ Jesus…had equal status with God!"* (Philippians 2:5 MSG).

Second, believe Jesus, while fully God, was at the same time fully human. *"The Word became flesh and made His dwelling among us. We have seen His glory, the glory of the one and only Son, who came from the Father!"* (John 1:14 NIV). And as Paul asserted, *"He made Himself nothing, by taking the very nature of a servant, being made in human likeness and being found in appearance as a man"* (Philippians 2:7,8 NIV).

Third, believe Jesus was sinless. *"God made Him who had no sin to be sin for us"* (II Corinthians 5:21 NIV). *"He committed no sin!"* (I Peter 2:22 NIV). *"…One, who has been tempted in every way, just as we are—yet He did not sin"* (Hebrews 4:15 NIV). This truth qualified Jesus as the only perfect candidate to be our substitute on the cross to make full payment for our sin and completely satisfy the holy justice of God.

Fourth, believe the Gospel of Jesus. *"By this gospel you are saved…that Christ died for our sins according to the Scripture; that He was buried; that He was raised on the third day according to the Scripture"* (I Corinthians 15:2-4 NIV).

Today's Crazy Big Idea: *"When you have lifted up the Son of Man, you will know that I AM!"* (John 8:28 NIV).

Today's Crazy Scripture: *"If you do not believe that I AM ...you will indeed die in your sins."* (John 8:24 NIV)

Today's Crazy Prayer Starter: "Dear Heavenly Father, I believe Jesus is as much God as You are God. I believe Your Son became human and lived a sinless life. I believe when He died on the cross, it was to pay for my sin. I believe You raised Jesus from the dead. Lord, help me live a life that is pleasing unto You. In Jesus' name, Amen.

"I AM" CRAZY

"I AM" CRAZY
DAY 23

"I tell you the truth, if anyone keeps My Word, He will never see death!" (John 8:51 NIV).

Jesus says it is possible for you NEVER to taste death! I emphasize "never" because when Jesus makes this astounding promise, He uses the strongest negative language possible. It is possible for you never, never, never to experience death.

This is an intriguing promise, particularly when you consider this quote. *"The stats on death are quite impressive; one out of one dies!"* -George Bernard Shaw

I have been thinking about death lately. I have been thinking about my death. Maybe death has not even been on your radar. This all started for me when I read an article in USA TODAY (January 23, 2016).

Before I tell you about this article, let me ask you this question. If you could know the exact day you're going to die, would you want to know?

The article I read in January in USA TODAY offered a web site that you could click on and discover the exact date of your death. So I did. I filled in the boxes relating to my life—birth date, gender, height, weight, whether or not I smoked; my outlook on life—pessimistic, normal, optimistic (Guess who lives longer—pessimists or optimists?).

I clicked the button that said, "Check your death." I found that according to this web site, I will die on Thursday, November 29, 2040. Whew! I've got another 24 years. I'm glad my death is not scheduled for a Monday. That's my day off.

Now I don't trust the accuracy of this death web site. Nor do I put my trust in George Bernard Shaw. When it comes to life and death issues, I'm putting my money on Jesus.

Here's why: Jesus is as much God, as God the Father is God! Jesus is the Son of the living God. When He talks about life and death issues, you can take it to the bank.

Consider this bold claim made by Jesus: *"'Just as the Father raises the dead and gives them life, even so the Son gives life to whom He pleases…I tell you the truth, whoever hears My Word and believes Him who sent Me has eternal life …He has crossed over from death to life!'"* (John 5:21,24 NIV).

This is not just about going to heaven after we die if we are Christ-followers. Maybe you sometimes wonder, "Just who is it that goes to heaven?" It is Christ-followers who go to heaven. We follow Christ into a real relationship with the Father. We follow Christ into regular worship. We follow Christ into prayer. We follow Christ into baptism. We follow Christ into the Word. We follow Christ with our money. We follow Christ with our time. We follow Christ with our willingness to serve others. We follow Christ with our love and compassion. Following Christ leads us right into heaven.

Now the great news is that when Jesus talks about crossing over from death to life, He's not just talking about going to heaven some day. He's talking about right now bringing dead stuff to life in you and in me.

If something goes dead in a marriage, Jesus can get that marriage crossed over from death to life. If something goes dead in us emotionally, Jesus can get our emotions crossed over from death to life. If something goes spiritually dead in our relationship with God, Jesus can get us crossed over from death into life. Dreams die. Hopes die. Sometimes it feels like our joy is dying; our love is dying; our faith is dying.

Jesus specializes in touching whatever is dead and making it come alive! What is it that has gone dead in your life that you need Jesus to touch and get it to come alive?

That's the offer Jesus makes in our text today. Jesus is in a heated debate with some really religious people who have something dead on the inside. Their religion has killed their relationship with God.

Here's the deal about having something go dead in our lives. The longer it stays dead, the more rotten it becomes. It comes out of us in anger, bitterness, ugliness, even hatred. It makes us want to control people and manipulate people to get our own way.

That's how John chapter 8 opens. These really religious people, with something dead on the inside, are trying to set a trap for Jesus, so they can have Him arrested. But they get caught in their own trap and walk away from Jesus roundly defeated. But then they come back after Jesus, this time even more viciously.

Have you ever had anyone treat you viciously in public? That's what these religious guys do to Jesus. They challenge

Him publicly, trying to humiliate Him. They attack His credibility. They attack His character. But Jesus stands up to their challenge. He re-directs their attacks by repeatedly confronting them with open declarations that He is the great "I AM," as much God as God the Father is God.

He straight up tells them that the reason they cannot recognize Him as the Son of God is because they don't know God.

Here's Jesus' closing argument, as He brings this debate to a climactic conclusion. He says, *"He who belongs to God hears what God says. The reason you do not hear is that you do not belong to God!"* (John 8:47 NIV).

The word Jesus uses for "hears" means to actively listen so as to understand and obey.

Jesus is telling these really rigorously religious guys, "You have a religion, but you don't have a relationship with God or you would grasp and live out His Word in your life."

This is the acid test of our relationship with God as well. Jesus bottom-lines it for us: We have God as our Heavenly Father; we are His children—co-heirs with Christ—when we actively listen to His Word, grasping what it means and applying it to our lives. This is a real relationship with God. This is the eternal life you live and never, never die.

Today's Crazy Big Idea: It is possible for you to never, never, never taste death!

Today's Crazy Scripture: *"I tell you the truth, whoever hears My Word and believes Him who sent Me has eternal life and will not be condemned; he has crossed over from death to life"* (John 5:24 NIV).

Today's Crazy Prayer Starter: "Dear Heavenly Father, You are my God. I belong to You. Help me grow in my longing for Your Word. Please open my mind to understand Scripture. Give me the wisdom to apply Your Word in my life. In Jesus' name, Amen!

"I AM" CRAZY

"I AM" CRAZY
DAY 24

What was your most recent painful conflict? Who was it with—your spouse, your kids, a co-worker? What was it about--politics, religion, sports, or a personal matter? Was it a major blow-up or a minor disagreement? Did you have a meltdown, or did you show emotional maturity? Did it happen on Facebook or behind closed doors?

I have two questions: 1. When you are in a conflict with someone, does it ever feel like the two of you are speaking different languages, like neither of you understands the other's perspective? 2. Have you ever had a conflict with God?

Here's a helpful hint when in conflict with the Lord: He speaks only the language of love. *"God is patient with you, not wanting anyone to perish, but everyone to come to repentance"* (II Peter 3:9 NIV).

So when listening to Jesus in seeming constant conflict with the really religious leaders of His day, we must hear His words as an intensely loving effort to break through their stubbornness and turn their hearts toward the truth of who He is.

So I hear the following words of Jesus as an urgent invitation: *"He who belongs to God hears (actively listens in order to understand and obey) what God says. The reason you do not hear is that you do not belong to God"* (John 8:47). Please belong to God!

Whatever Jesus intended, His words were like lighting a fuse to a powder keg. These really religious guys go off on Jesus, like a bunch of angry, mud-slinging politicians. *"The Jews then said, 'That clinches it. We were right all along when we called You a Samaritan and said You were crazy—demon-possessed!'"* (John 8:48 MSG).

There is an escalation to every conflict. This one is getting out of hand. The Jews are using what to them is the worst kind of racial slur, calling Jesus a Samaritan. Then as happens in most escalating arguments, they demonize Jesus, "You're evil."

But Jesus refuses to lower Himself and play their brand of dirty politics. Jesus refuses to attack back in kind. He takes the conversation to the highest level possible as He shifts the focus on to God. *"'I am not possessed by a demon,' said Jesus, 'but I honor My Father and you dishonor Me. I am not seeking glory for Myself, but there is One who seeks it!'"* (John 8:49,50 NIV).

Jesus gives us a glimpse here at how to have a real relationship with God. Jesus says, "I aim at honoring the Father. The Father aims at glorifying Me." That's how it works in our lives. I aim at honoring the Father in my family. The Father aims at glorifying my family. You aim at honoring the Father in your work. The Father aims at glorifying your work. I aim at honoring the Father with my finances. The Father aims at glorifying my finances. You aim at honoring the Father by serving others. The Father aims at glorifying your service to others.

This unending cycle of honor and glory is what a real relationship with Jesus produces. I love the way Paul proclaims it: *"Christ in you, the hope of glory!"* (Colossians 1:27 NIV).

DAY 24

This glory can begin right now and can carry us into an unending, unlimited experience of God's glory in heaven.

But there's more here. Jesus does more than honor God. **Jesus offers God's grace!** Jesus offers to personally touch what is dead in these religious guys and bring it alive. *"I tell you the truth, if anyone keeps My Word, he will never see death!"* (John 8:51 NIV).

Jesus uses the phrase, "I tell you the truth," 25 times in the book of John alone. It's like putting a big exclamation point at the beginning of a sentence. It's like a huge heads up that the next thing He says is of incredible importance.

I love the invitation part of what Jesus offers. When Jesus says, "anyone," it's like throwing His arms open to everyone—both genders, all colors, all cultures. It's not about having so much education or so much money or the right social connections or the right political stance. It is unconditional acceptance in its purest form.

But "anyone" says more than that. "Anyone" means that each one must take initiative themselves. It is their personal responsibility. Jesus is saying, "You are personally invited to keep My Word. But no one can do it for you. You must do it for yourself."

The word "keeps" does not mean "to possess" God's Word, but to practice God's Word.

It's not something we practice in terms of our right behavior. It's something we practice in terms of our right belief.

So what is right belief as it relates to Jesus? Paul lays it out simple and plain. *"By this Gospel (Good News) you are saved, if you hold firmly to the Word I preached to you. Otherwise, you have believed in vain. For what I received I passed on to you as of first importance: that Christ died for our sins according to the Scriptures, that He was buried, that He was raised on the third day according to the Scriptures"* (I Corinthians 15:2-4).

Nothing is more important than getting this belief right. It has eternal implications for your life. By believing this Good News about Jesus, you are saved from the deadly power of sin, the grave, and hell itself. If you believe something or someone else has the power to deliver you from death, your belief is in vain.

First, you must believe that Jesus is the Christ, the anointed One of God. Second, you believe He died on the cross in your place to take the full punishment for your sins. You believe this truth is the fulfillment of numerous Bible prophesies (ie. Psalm 22, 41:9; Isaiah 50:6, 53:4-7, 9, 12; Zechariah 11:12,13, 12:10). You believe that Jesus was fully, physically dead, so He was buried. This is why we join Him in His burial by baptism. And you believe that on the third day, God raised Jesus from the dead, just as had been prophesied in Scripture (i.e., Psalm 16:10; 40:2; Hosea 6:2; Job 19:25).

Right belief in Jesus brings you into right, conflict-free relationship with your saving God.

Today's Crazy Big Idea: Right belief in Jesus brings you into right, conflict-free relationship with your saving God.

Today's Crazy Scripture: *"God is patient with you, not wanting anyone to perish, but everyone to come to repentance!"* (II Peter 3:9 NIV).

Today's Crazy Prayer Starter: "Dear Heavenly Father, I want to aim my life at honoring You. I believe that You loved me so, You gave Your one and only Son, Jesus, to die for my sins. I believe You raised Jesus from the dead. I believe that Christ in me is my hope of glorified living. Praise Your name! For Your sake, Amen."

"I AM" CRAZY

"I AM" CRAZY
DAY 25

I have made some terrible deals in my time. The worst and the most painful usually relate to trading cars. I have this mental condition. When I think about buying a car, my brain cells die off in appalling number.

My most horrible car deal happened with my son, Wilky. Together, we had a few thousand dollars (which is a lot of money to us) to buy his first car. Wilky found the car on Craig's List (I know. I know. Dumb move. But I'm telling you, I have a mental condition.). I contacted the owner and made an appointment to see the car. We were to meet him at a car wash in Rockford. When we got there, Wilky really liked the car. Price-wise, it was a great deal. The car had no license plates, so I couldn't take it to our mechanic as I had planned. I drove it around the carwash, acting like I knew what I was doing. I asked a few pertinent questions. I believed every lie the owner told me. We gave him our money. He gave us the title. We went to the DMV to get license plates. We went back to get the car and take it to our mechanic, who tells me the transmission is shot. A rebuilt one will cost as much as we paid for the car. I tried to contact the car's owner only to find out I'd been given a fake identity and a fake phone number. I wanted to break every one of the Ten Commandments on the guy's head.

So if you ever think of yourself as lacking in intelligence, think of me, and you'll feel like a genius. Now that you know my dumbest deal, let me tell you about my most brilliant trade. It has nothing to do with cars. It has everything to do with Christ.

Here's the deal of all deals. The offer I found totally irresistible. When I surrendered my life to Jesus, I got a 4-point deal with a promise of Scripture for each point. First, everything wrong with me was put on Him and everything right with Jesus was put on me (*"God put the wrong on Him, who never did anything wrong, so we could be put right with God!"* II Corinthians 5:21 MSG). Second, God now refuses to be angry with me for anything. On the cross, Jesus bore all the wrath of God due me for my sin (*"How much more will we be saved from God's wrath through Him!"* Romans 5:9 NIV). Third, now I will never be judged by God (*"God doesn't treat us as our sins deserve, nor pay us in full for our wrongs."* Psalm 103:10 MSG). Fourth, I will never be condemned by God (*"There is now no condemnation for those who are in Christ Jesus!"* Romans 8:1 NIV).

Here's the incredible deal Jesus offers to the really religious guys: *"If anyone keeps My Word, he will never see death"* (John 8:51 NIV).

They turn Him down flat. *"The Jews exclaimed, 'Now we know You are demon-possessed! Abraham died and so did the prophets, yet You say that if anyone keeps Your Word, he will never taste death. Are You greater than our ancestor Abraham? He died and so did the prophets. Who do You think You are?'"* (John 8:52,53 NIV).

"Who do You think You are?" Jesus loves to be confronted

DAY 25

with this question. He loves to answer it by declaring Himself as the great **"I AM!"**—I AM the Light of the world!

I AM the Bread of Life. I AM the Good Shepherd. I AM the Way, the Truth, and the Life. I AM the Resurrection and the Life. I AM God, and I do what God does.

But before Jesus directly tells these Jews who He is, He gives them a huge hint. *"Your ancestor Abraham rejoiced at the thought of seeing My day; he saw it and was glad!"* (John 8:56 NIV). Abraham, looking down from heaven, is jumping up and down with joy, cheering for Jesus and hoping that these dead-on-the-inside religious guys will believe.

It's not going to happen. They blast Jesus with unbelief. *"'You are not yet fifty years old,' the Jews said to Jesus, 'and You have seen Abraham!'"* (John 8:57 NIV).

Jesus has them right where He wants them. It's time for another "I AM" declaration that He is God. *"'I tell you the truth,' Jesus answered, 'before Abraham was born, I AM!' At this they picked up stones to stone Him, but Jesus hid Himself, slipping away from the temple grounds"* (John 8:58,59 NIV).

The religious leaders know Jesus is claiming to be God. They want to kill Him for it. They know Jesus is claiming more than equality with God. Jesus is claiming He can do what God does. The religious leaders know the Scriptures. They want to see Jesus dead, before they see Him as the fulfillment of God-made prophecies and promises, like these by Isaiah.

"I am I AM, and apart from Me there is no Savior! I have revealed and saved and proclaimed!" (Isaiah 43:11 Septuagint, a Greek translation of the Old Testament).

"From ancient of days I AM! No one can deliver out of My hand! When I act, who can reverse it?" (Isaiah 43:13 Septuagint).

"I AM" CRAZY

"I, even I AM, who blots out your transgressions, for My own sake, and remembers your sin no more!" (Isaiah 43:25 Septuagint).

The very implications that made the religious hate Jesus make me love Him with all my heart and follow Him with all my life. There is no Savior but Jesus. No one can deliver out of His hand. I'm safe and secure in His constant care. He forgives forever.

Jesus, the Son of the living God, came to our planet with an outstanding offer: *"Let's make a deal,"* beautifully captured in this announcement: *"The Father has given Me all these things to do and say. This is a unique Father/Son operation, coming out of Father and Son intimacies and knowledge. No one knows the Son the way the Father does, nor the Father the way the Son does. But I'm not keeping it to Myself; I'm ready to go over it line by line with anyone willing to listen. Are you tired? Worn out? Burned out on religion? Come to Me. Get away with Me and you'll recover your life. I'll show you how to take a real rest. Walk with Me and work with Me—watch how I do it. Learn the unforced rhythms of grace. I won't lay anything heavy or ill-fitting on you. Keep company with Me and you'll learn to live freely and lightly.* (Matthew 11:27-30 MSG).

I likely deserved every bad deal I've ever made. I purchased impulsively. I did not do enough research. I bought the seller's spiel hook, line, and sinker. Dang it.

There's no way I ever deserved the greatest deal I ever made, trading in my sins to a faithful, compassionate Savior, who cleansed me of all guilt and shame and favored me with His great goodness. *"It is by grace (I) have been saved through faith--and this is not from (myself); it is the gift of God!"* (Ephesians 2:8).

DAY 25

Today's Crazy Big Idea: There is no Savior like the eternal Jesus. When He acts, no one can reverse it. We are safe and secure in His constant care.

Today's Crazy Big Scripture: *"I, even I AM, who blots out your transgressions, for My own sake, and remembers your sins no more"* (Isaiah 43:25 Greek Septuagint of O.T.).

Today's Crazy Big Prayer Starter: "Dear Jesus, I am willing to listen to You. Please go over Your Word with me line by line. I want to walk with You and keep company with You. You alone have the words of Life. In Your name and for Your sake, Amen."

"I AM" CRAZY

"I AM" CRAZY
DAY 26

You find out that you're unemployed. You find out that you're going to give birth to a special needs baby. Your doctor says that it's stage 4 cancer. A loved one passes away. You find out that your son's been arrested. You find out that your daughter has a mental illness. Your parents both have Alzheimer's. All you can think to say is, "I have never felt so helpless and alone."

Have you ever been through something so hard, so hurtful, so painfully impossible that you feel stranded on a lonely island of helplessness? If you haven't been there, you will be. And when you are, this is what you have to remind yourself: **Jesus sees what I'm going through, and He wants me to know He is with me and for me.**

Let me explain by taking you into a day in the life of Jesus. *"As Jesus passed by, he saw a man, who was blind from his birth!"* (John 9:1 KJV).

Two staggering realities jump out at us from this one sentence. The first is this man was born blind. His dark disability was considered incurable. It was a painful impossibility. People who had lost their sight had regained it. Jesus had healed people who, for whatever reason, had become blind. But no one had ever healed a man born blind. He was thought to be beyond help, hopelessly confined to a lifetime of absolute darkness.

The second staggering reality is this: Jesus is always passing in close proximity to those in desperate need. Jesus is passing by you right now—whatever your need. He's as close as the air you breathe. *"The LORD is close to the brokenhearted!"* (Psalm 34:18 NIV).

Do you want to see how close Jesus is? Imagine the scene with me. The blind man is seated with his back against a wall on a busy, narrow street. He sits cross-legged to keep his feet out of the way of all the hustle and bustle of people. His head moves from side to side, separating all the sounds surging around him. He hears everything, but he sees nothing. In the blackness of his blindness, he begs for money.

Jesus sees the blind man in his painful impossibility. Coming close, Jesus kneels beside the blind man. The blind man senses the presence of Jesus and hears the words that will change His life forever, as Jesus declares, *"While I am in the world, I AM the Light of the World!"* (John 9:5 NIV).

Jesus is down in the dirt with this blind man, declaring Himself to be God. When Jesus claimed to be the Light of the World, the blind man's mind would immediately have jumped to these promises of God: *"The LORD is my Light!"* (Psalm 27:1); *"The LORD will be your everlasting Light!"* (Isaiah 60:19); *"By His light I walk through darkness!"* (Job 29:3); *"When I sit in darkness, the LORD will be a light to me"* (Micah 7:8).

While these promises were rising up in the blind man's mind, Jesus spat in the dirt and used His saliva to make mud. Jesus took the mud and put it on the man's blind eyes. *"'Go,'*

DAY 26

Jesus told him, 'wash in the pool of Siloam' (this word means, 'the one sent'). So the man went and washed and came home seeing!" (John 9:7 NIV).

Why does Jesus command this blind man to go to this special pool when obviously he could have washed the mud off his eyes just about anywhere there was water? The word "Siloam" means "the one sent." Get this. Twenty-seven times in John's account Jesus calls Himself "the One sent."

This whole process was designed by Jesus, so the blind man would know exactly who provided his unprecedented, miraculous healing. The man, being blind, cannot see the face of Jesus. Jesus uses the mud made by His saliva, so the blind man will know that the One, declaring Himself as the Light of the World, is the One who healed him. It's for the same reason that Jesus sends him to the pool of Siloam. Jesus is the One sent. Jesus wants the man to know that there's nothing magic about the water. The pool is simply meant to point to Jesus, the One sent. The pool is Jesus. The picture is this: the blind man is to go to Jesus, be washed in Jesus, and thus experience miraculous healing in relationship to Jesus.

This is a beautiful picture of baptism. I always want people to know when I baptize them, there's no special power in the water. What's special is that they are being bathed in Christ. Their sins are washed away (Acts 22:16 NIV).

When you experience baptism, you experience Jesus. Just as the blind man went and washed and came home seeing. So you come to Jesus. You are washed in Him. You come home to God, seeing and living life in a whole new way.

Paul says it this way: *"Don't you know that all of us who were baptized into Christ Jesus were baptized into His death? We were* *therefore buried with Him through baptism into death in order that, just as Christ was raised from the dead through the glory of the Father, **we too may live a new life!**"* (Romans 6:3,4 NIV).

Peter says it this way: *"This water symbolizes baptism that now saves you also—not the removal of dirt from the body but the pledge of a clear conscience to God. It saves you by the resurrection of Jesus Christ!"* (I Peter 3:21 NIV).

This is the very reason why the people in our church get all fired up when they see someone baptized. There's always a spiritual excitement in the air. But what happens in our church cannot compare to what happens in heaven. Angels sing and dance. Jesus jumps for joy and shouts out the name of the person just baptized. Remember His promise: *"Whoever acknowledges Me before others, I will also acknowledge before My Father in heaven"* (Matthew 10:32 NIV).

God the Father smiles with delight over the person being baptized and whispers into their soul, *"You are My beloved child in whom I am well pleased."* The Holy Spirit tops off the whole experience by filling the person to the full with the fullness of God.

If Jesus brought healing to a helpless man with a painful impossibility, He can do the same for you. He wants to whisper over your life right now, *"I AM the Light of the World!"* Never stop saying to yourself, **"Jesus sees what I'm going through and He wants me to know He is with me and for me!"**

DAY 26

Today's Crazy Big Idea: Jesus sees what I'm going through, and He wants me to know He is with me and for me.

Today's Crazy Scripture: *"The LORD is close to the brokenhearted!"* (Psalm 34:18 NIV).

Today's Crazy Prayer Starter: "Dear Lord, please shine Your light into the dark places in my life. I know that You are the Christ, the Son of the living God. You cared enough to die for my sins, so You care enough to help me through my darkness. You conquered death itself, so You can give me victory over my struggle. In Your name, Amen."

"I AM" CRAZY

"I AM" CRAZY
DAY 27

Who is it in your life, who loves to rain on your spiritual parade? You develop a keen interest in Jesus or you're flat-out, falling in love with Jesus. You have a growing sense of His presence and a keen appreciation for what Jesus has done in your life. But just as you get a fresh enthusiasm for Jesus, someone in your life gets a fierce antagonism toward you and Jesus. They don't think twice about going ballistic about Jesus in general and Christians in particular. These folks are dark clouds, storming on your faith.

If you know what that feels like, you know what our newly-sighted man was about to experience. He feels like something sensational has happened in his life. He thinks he has been touched by the power of God. But people around him don't think he deserves to be blessed. In fact, some really religious person got all bent out of shape and called in the religion police. As they began to interrogate the man who could now see, a huge crowd of people gathered.

When the man who'd been blind explains how he had received his sight, the religion police get their noses all up in the air and start slamming Jesus in front of the crowd: "This fellow

"I AM" CRAZY

is not from God or He would not be doing this kind of work on our holy day."

But people in the crowd shout back, "No run-of-the-mill sinner could perform a miracle like this." Then the religion police started saying this recently healed man had never been blind in the first place. They called in his parents. "Is this your son?" "Yes." "Was he born blind?" "Yes." "How is it that now he can see?" But these parents were so intimidated by the religion police they would only say, "Hey, we're staying out of this."

So the religion police grabbed the newly-sighted man and demanded, "Tell the truth so help you God. If it was Jesus who did this, we know He is a wicked sinner." The healed man said, "All I know is—I was blind, and now I can see." They started cussing this guy up one side and down the other. Finally, they said, "You are out. You are shunned. You are banned from ever being part of our life, our community, or our religion."

Have you ever been in this newly-sighted guy's place? Through no fault of your own, people shut you out. They put you down. They tell you off, and then they shut you out. They want other people to shut you out as well. The people you think would come to your defense, like this guy's parents, throw you under the bus.

I guarantee you that's when Jesus comes passing your way. That's what happened to the newly sighted, recently banned, totally shunned guy. Jesus strides right back into the scene and comes to the man's side. I think Jesus puts His arm around the guy, gives him a big smile and says, "No worries. I've got your back."

That's your reality right now. Whether you feel it or not, it is a fact. Jesus is as close to you right now as the air you breathe. He has His arm wrapped affectionately around your shoulder. He's trying to smile His love and confidence into your heart. Even if, like the religion police, you don't believe that Jesus is God, He is irresistibly drawn to you right now. He wants to speak into your heart right now about how the love of God works.

This is how He did it for the crowd, the religion police, and the newly-sighted guy under his arm. Jesus tells a story. *"I tell you the truth, the man who does not enter the sheep pen by the gate, but climbs in by some other way, is a thief and a robber"* (John 10:1 NIV).

As Jesus began His story, everyone in His audience had the same image in mind. In that day at the center of a village was a sheep pen. All the shepherds of the village kept their sheep together in the same pen overnight. When they came back to the village in the evening, after a day of leading the sheep from one pasture to another, they herded their sheep back into the pen with everyone else's sheep. All the shepherds kicked in some cash and paid a night watchman to guard all the sheep.

The watchman stood guard at the gate of the sheep pen. But if he was not diligent or if he fell asleep, a thief could sneak into the sheep pen. The Greek word here for "thief" is "kleptas," from which we get our word, "kleptomaniac," meaning "one who steals." But the Greek word for "robber" does not mean "to steal." It means "to slaughter."

The sheep in this story represent us. Jesus is warning us there are people in our lives who want to steal or kill our relationship with Jesus. They will say hurtful things and do hateful things in an effort to put our faith to death.

The people listening to Jesus knew exactly what would happen next in this shepherding business. First thing in the morning, each shepherd would come to lead his sheep out to pasture. Here's how Jesus tells it: *"The man who enters by the gate is the shepherd of his sheep. The watchman opens the gate for him, and the sheep listen to his voice. He calls his own sheep by name and leads them out. When he's brought out all his own, he goes on ahead of them and his sheep follow him, because they know his voice"* (John 10:2-4 NIV).

This is huge. If we are the sheep, Jesus is our shepherd. He knows us. He knows our lives inside-and out. He sees us, calls us by name, and offers to take the lead in life.

The shepherd would always go first, ahead of his sheep. If there was a nest of snakes, he got there first and steered all the sheep to safety. If there was a wolf, the shepherd was out in front to deal with the wolf before the wolf could deal with the sheep.

This is a beautiful image of our Jesus. He goes first. We can confidently follow Jesus, knowing He will take care of any wolves or snakes who try to do damage to our faith.

If we keep following Jesus, He will inevitably lead us into heaven, where He is both Lamb and Shepherd to His people. *"The Lamb at the center of the throne will be their Shepherd; He will lead them to springs of living water. And God will wipe away every tear from their eyes"* (Revelation 7:17 NIV).

Today's Crazy Big Idea: If we keep following Jesus, He will inevitably lead us into heaven, where He is both Lamb and Shepherd to His people.

Today's Crazy Scripture: *"The Lamb at the center of the throne will be their Shepherd; He will lead them to springs of living water. And God will wipe away every tear from their eyes"* (Revelation 7:17 NIV).

Today's Crazy Prayer Starter: "Dear Lord, You are my Shepherd. You are everything I need. You are my rest in the stress of life. You restore my soul. You guide me through all chaos and confusion. I pray for those who do not know You. Their effort to weaken my faith only serves to make it stronger. I love You, Lord. Praise Your Name, Amen.

"I AM" CRAZY

"I AM" CRAZY
DAY 28

"What the heck!" Jesus was blowing their minds. It wasn't so much the miracle, though it was unprecedented, restoring the sight of a man born blind. Who had ever heard of anything like that? But by now, Jesus and miracles seemed like a package deal. After all, there was talk of water being turned into wine. It was said He calmed vicious storms with one word of peace. There was even an incredible story of Jesus walking on water. Thousands had witnessed Him turn a little boy's lunch into a meal for a multitude.

It wasn't even the half dozen times Jesus had declared His equality with God. This time was different. This time He was not saying something humongous, like "I AM the Light of the world" or "I AM the Bread of Life." This time, it was something unbelievably insignificant and humble. Jesus had just declared Himself to be a shepherd, willing to lay down His own life for His followers. Who had ever heard of a God like that?

Jesus compared Himself to a shepherd. Shepherds were anonymous nobodies. The most outstanding attribute of a shepherd was how deeply he loved his sheep. A good shepherd would always be willing to sacrifice himself for his sheep.

"I AM" CRAZY

It would be awesome to have a God who was like a shepherd, guiding and providing, protective and patient, loving and kind. Who wouldn't want to have a God like that? But there is a condition. We have to be willing to follow. We have to listen to His voice.

Good sheep follow their good shepherd. There must be a relationship between Jesus, our Shepherd, and us, His sheep. So this is not just about Jesus knowing us; it's equally important that we know Jesus—that we know Him well enough to recognize His voice; that we know Him well enough to trust that where He leads is best for us.

When we listen to His voice regarding our relationships, we can trust Him to lead us into what is best for our families and our friendships. When we listen to His voice regarding our money, we can trust Him to lead us into what is best for us financially. When we listen to His voice regarding our emotions, we can trust Jesus to lead us into joy, peace, hope, and love.

Our church leadership is reading a book (*With*, Skye Jethani) about being in real relationship with God. In the first chapter, the author uses two images that spoke to me. The first graphic concerns an adage we've all heard: "all religions lead to God." In the book, there is a mountain pictured, with God at the top. It shows religion arrows A, B, C, and D all leading to God. But the author points out that this is a lie.

The truth is in the second image. It depicts religion arrows A,B,C, and D all leading down the mountain and away from God. The fact is all religions lead away from God. Only Jesus is the way into a real relationship with God. All other voices calling to us are strangers, thieves, and robbers.

DAY 28

There are all kinds of religions that can lead people away from God. Money can be a religion. Work can be a religion. Sports can be a religion. Even our families can be a religion. All these things are actually good. But if they lead us away from God, they are strangers, thieves, and robbers.

This is the truth Jesus holds up as He climaxes His teaching. He's still got His arm around the newly, miraculously sighted man. There's still a crowd gathered. The religion police still want to arrest Him. But Jesus still wants to show all of them what the love of God looks like and how the love of God works. Jesus wants to take every last one of them into His arms. Jesus has His arms opened wide to you right now.

"Jesus said again, 'I tell you the truth, I AM the Gate for the sheep!" (John 10:7 NIV).

But how can Jesus be both the shepherd and the gate? The people listening to Jesus that day knew exactly what He meant. They knew that when a shepherd took his sheep out to pasture, he often had to go a great distance. If he led his sheep so far that he couldn't get back to the village by evening, then he built a makeshift sheep pen, where the sheep could bed down at night. But this make-shift sheep pen had no gate like the one in the village, so the shepherd himself became the gate.

Let me explain. As the sun was setting, the shepherd would call his sheep into the enclosure he had built. But the shepherd himself does not go into the sheep pen. He stands at the entrance with his shepherd's rod. He held his rod low enough to stop each sheep. He made each sheep pass him in single file. Then he would carefully and tenderly inspect each sheep one by one. If he found a weakness, he would do whatever was necessary to care for it.

This is how Jesus personally cares for you. You are the apple of His eye. He tenderly looks over your life as if you were the only sheep in His flock. If He sees weakness, He offers His strength. If He sees despair, He offers His hope. If He sees stress, He offers His peace.

Even when you've been wayward, He offers you mercy. When you fail, He forgives you. When you fall down, He picks you up. To prove that all this is true between Jesus and one of His sheep, He makes Himself the gate for the sheep.

Did you catch that? Jesus said, *"I AM the Gate FOR the sheep!"* (John 10:7 NIV). That little three-letter word is everything. *"Christ died FOR our sins!"* (I Corinthians 15:3 NIV). *"Greater love has no one than this, that he lay down his life FOR his friends!"* (John 15:13 NIV).

When a shepherd out in the wilderness built a makeshift shelter for his sheep, it had an entrance but no gate. The shepherd became the gate. With each sheep carefully inspected and safely inside the fold, the shepherd laid down across the entrance. No sheep could get out without crossing his body. No predator could enter without crossing His body. The shepherd literally laid his body down for His sheep.

Jesus, our Shepherd and Gate, makes it possible for us to enter the presence of God by *"...a new and living way opened for us through...His body!"* (Hebrews 10:20 NIV).

Today's Crazy Big Idea: Jesus tenderly cares for you as if you were the only sheep in His flock.

Today's Crazy Scripture: *"I AM the Gate! Anyone who enters through Me will be saved. I am come that they might have life, and that they might have it more abundantly!"* (John 10:9,10 NIV, KJV).

Today's Crazy Prayer Starter: "Dear LORD, I am blown away by Your willingness to love me to the fullest extent. Please help me to grasp the height, the depth, the length, and the width of Your love for me. I love having You as my Shepherd and Gate. Amen!"

"I AM" CRAZY

"I AM" CRAZY
DAY 29

Has life ever hammered you with a painful, unpleasant surprise, turning ugly in no time? A marriage can turn ugly in no time. A friendship can turn ugly in no time. Parenting can turn ugly in no time. Your health can turn ugly. Your finances can turn ugly. Cancer is ugly. Divorce is ugly. Unemployment is ugly. Abuse is ugly. Losing a loved one is the ugliest. Depression is ugly. Addiction is ugly. **Life can turn ugly in no time. That's why we need the beauty of Jesus *all* the time!**

Here's a scenario I've seen played out in my life all too often. I can be a master at multiplying my own problems. If life turns ugly, I can make it uglier.

For instance, when we were embroiled in our efforts to adopt Lovia, painful problems popped up at every turn. A huge, on-going obstacle was a lack of funds. There was a pressurized moment when the adoption was dead in the water unless we could come up with $2,000. There was no way. We were already adoption poor—no money.

I was flying out to Colorado for a conference. I didn't want to go. It seemed like the worst time to be away from home. During the flight, I felt claustrophobic on the plane. All the stress of our struggle was suffocating. My thoughts started going dark: "I'm a failure. Nothing ever works out for me. Even when I do my best, it's never enough."

Now I had two problems—a lack of money and a load of discouragement. That's when the worry started. This made three problems. "Would our lawyer bail on us? Would our adoption papers go to the bottom of the pile? If we didn't have enough money for this part, how would we come up with the funds needed to finish the adoption?"

I wanted to talk to God about all this. But I did more pouting than praying. I was kicking myself because I had agreed to preach for a church before the conference. I kicked myself again because I wasn't being paid to speak. If I wasn't careful, I'd have a bad attitude to put on my pile of problems.

The next day, as I drove away from the church, I was tired from preaching and all the people interaction. I just wanted to get to my motel and crash. That's when it occurred to me. A man had stopped me out in the church parking lot. He put a folded-up check in my hand, which I stuck in my pocket. He said, "My wife and I have never been able to have children. We want to help you make this little girl your daughter."

I remembered the check. I dug in my pocket. I unfolded it to see that the check was made out for $2,000. There's no way this generous couple could have known they were gifting us with the exact amount of money we needed to keep the adoption going.

I had to pull off to the side of the road. I was overcome. I put my face in my hands and wept with joy and gratitude. I called Deby with the unbelievably good news.

Before I pulled back onto the highway, I counseled myself: "David, where's your faith? God has been at work to your good all along. If you'd just waited patiently on Him, you could have skipped the fear, worry, the dark thinking, and discouragement. From now on, when life turns ugly, don't turn inward with self-pity; turn upward with praise."

That was not the last wonder God worked in our behalf. He kept at it until the adoption was finalized. One less girl in an orphanage meant the first girl in the Clark family.

Life can turn ugly in no time. That's why we need the beauty of Jesus all the time.

Sooner or later, life always turns ugly. When it does, Jesus wants to introduce Himself to us in a very special way. He says, *"I AM the Good Shepherd!"* (John 10:11 NIV).

It's easy to miss the full force of this incredible promise in our English. This is how it is literally translated from the original Greek:. *"I AM THE Shepherd—THE good One!"*

I emphasized "the" both times because these are both definite articles. Jesus is not claiming to be just another shepherd or a good one but THE shepherd—THE good one.

This is another case of Jesus emphasizing His equality with God. In Jewish religious thought of that day, the title Shepherd was synonymous with God. Let me give examples from Scripture to help us see the beauty of Jesus, our good Shepherd.

See how deeply personal our Jesus is: *"The LORD is my Shepherd!"* (Psalm 23:1 NIV).

When life turns ugly, we can cry out to Him in prayer: *"Hear us, Shepherd…You who lead (us) like a flock. You sit enthroned be-*

tween the cherubim. Shine forth! Awaken Your might; come and save us!" (Psalm 80:1,2 NIV).

Here's how God Himself says it: *"'You are My sheep. The sheep of My pasture are people and I am your God,' declares the Sovereign LORD!"* (Ezekiel 34:31 NIV).

We can claim the protection and provision of our Shepherd. *"For He is our God and we are the people of His pasture, the flock under His care"* (Psalm 95:7 NIV).

The LORD, our Shepherd, is worthy of worship. *"We, Your people, the sheep of Your pasture, will praise You forever!"* (Psalm 79:13 NIV).

With the LORD as our Shepherd, His Kingdom is ours. *"Do not be afraid, little flock, for the Father has been pleased to give you His Kingdom!"* (Luke 12:32 NIV).

See the beauty of our Shepherd. He carries the weak. He holds us close to his heart. He slows down to go at our pace. *"He tends His flock like a shepherd; He gathers the lambs in His arms and carries them close to His heart. He gently leads those who have young"* (Isaiah 40:11 NIV).

Life can turn ugly in no time; that's why we need the beauty of our Jesus—THE Shepherd, THE good One—all the time!

Today's Crazy Big Idea: Life can turn ugly in no time. That's why we need the beauty of Jesus all the time.

Today's Crazy Scripture: *"I AM the good Shepherd. The good Shepherd lays down His life for His sheep"* (John 10:11 NIV).

Today's Crazy Prayer Starter: "Hear us, Shepherd, You who lead us like a flock. Shine forth. Awaken Your might and save us. For Your sake, Amen."

"I AM" CRAZY

"I AM" CRAZY
DAY 30

Here's one of my tattoo-worthy life mottos: "If something is good, more of it is better!"

I know that right now many of you are trying to poke holes in my little life truism. You want to tell me that ice cream is good. But more of it will make me bloat up like a beached whale. Personally, I'm willing to take that risk. So you say, "TV is good; but more and more of it and my brain cells will start to die." I say, "Huh? I don't understand."

Okay, okay. Maybe you have a point. But here's a motto that merits being tattooed on your heart forever. **More and more of Jesus, THE Shepherd, THE GOOD One, is better than the best!**

Jesus is very specific and particular when He declares Himself the good Shepherd. There are two words for "good" in the Greek language. One is "agathos," from which we get the woman's name, Agatha. Agathos means "nice, kind." I think that's what we often mistakenly mean when we say, "God is good." Like God is so nice, so kind. Like God is a 90 year old grandmother. But our world is so broken and so sin-damaged that a nice, "Mr. Rogers" kind of Jesus would do us no good at all.

Jesus chooses a different, very unique word to describe Himself as the good Shepherd. Jesus uses the word, "kalos." It's a powerfully profound word. It means "beautiful, excellent, all-surpassing."

So this is what Jesus actually claimed and this is how He wants us to know Him: *"I AM God, THE Shepherd, THE beautiful, excellent, all-surpassing One!"*

Do you know what it is about Jesus that establishes Him as the beautiful, excellent, and all surpassing One? He lays it out in His very next breath: *"The good Shepherd lays down His life for His sheep!"* (John 10:11 NIV).

It is the sacrifice of His life on the cross that absolutely establishes Jesus as THE beautiful One, THE excellent One, THE all-surpassing One.

What excites me about this is that Jesus is showing us how to be fully ready when life turns ugly. This is how we have the beauty of Jesus all the time.

In these three words describing Jesus, we find a triple antidote for the ugliness of life. **When life turns ugly, we triumph over it as we worship the beauty of Jesus!**

This is why being in worship every weekend with the Body of Christ to celebrate the beauty of Christ is so essential for growing stronger than any ugliness life can throw at you. When you neglect the weekly experience of offering worship to Jesus, you get weaker day by day. Then when life hammers you, as it always will, instead of being able to stand strong, you crumble under the pressure like an empty bag of potato chips.

This is why it is such a tragedy that the average church-goer in America is present for worship only once a month. They claim a relationship with Jesus and could be stronger in life

DAY 30

than all others—emotionally, mentally, relationally, spiritually. But by not making worship a weekly priority, they are as easily devastated by the ugliness of life as people who don't even believe in Jesus. We are weakened without weekly worship. Genuine worshippers have the spiritual strength to turn any trouble into triumph.

This is why it breaks my heart to hear people believe Satan's lie: "You don't have to go to church to be a Christian." Worshipping the beauty of Jesus is what keeps you in right relationship with Jesus. Worship the beauty of the Shepherd, and then He goes ahead of you, working everything together for the good.

Worship the beauty of the Shepherd, for He is able to do immeasurably more than all you can ask or even imagine according to His power that is at work within you.

There's more. Our good Shepherd is excellent. **When life turns ugly, we triumph over it as we thank God for the excellence of Jesus!**

The excellence of something speaks to its perfection. This is Jesus, our Shepherd. He is utterly perfect. This is everything to us. Where we have failed miserably in life, Jesus flourished flawlessly. He battled His way tenaciously through every temptation until He had victoriously achieved a sinless life. He knew no sin and did no sin. That made Him the only qualified candidate to sacrifice His own perfect life as full payment for our sins.

Here's something we all know: No one's perfect except Jesus. But here's the wild thing. When you believe Jesus is the Son of the living God -- that He died to pay for your sins and God raised Him from the dead -- you are made perfect in

Christ. All the deserved consequences of your sin are applied to Jesus and all the undeserved benefits of His excellent perfection are applied to your life.

The Bible says it this way: *"God made Him who had no sin to be sin FOR us, so that in Him we might become the righteousness of God!"* (II Corinthians 5:21 NIV). Our good Shepherd is beautiful. He is utterly perfect and willing to share His perfection with us. He even perfects our painful, personal imperfections. But He's even more. Our good Shepherd is all-surpassing. **When life turns ugly, we experience the beauty of Jesus, as we lay down our lives for our all-surpassing Jesus!**

Jesus served us fully by freely laying down His life on the cross. But we don't have to die on a cross to experience His beauty. We lay down our lives fully by freely doing ministry in His name—serving children, feeding the hungry, loving our neighbors, giving generously and faithfully, helping the hurting, creating a welcoming environment in our weekend worship and telling others how all-surpassing our beautiful Jesus truly is.

"Real believers are the ones the Spirit of God leads to work away at this ministry, filling the air with Christ's praise as we do it!" (Philippians 3:3 MSG).

DAY 30

Today's Crazy Big Idea: Jesus is our Shepherd, the beautiful One, the excellent One, the all-surpassing One.

Today's Crazy Scripture: *"This is how we come to understand and experience love: Christ sacrificed His life for us. This is why we ought to live sacrificially for our fellow believers"* (I John 3:16 MSG).

Today's Crazy Prayer Starter: Dear Jesus, You are my Shepherd, the beautiful One, the excellent One, the all-surpassing One. You served me by laying down your life to pay for my sin. Please use me. Show me ways to serve others in Your name, filling the air with Your praise. For Your sake, Amen!

"I AM" CRAZY

"I AM" CRAZY
DAY 31

We all need Jesus because life is full of trouble!

We all know that some trouble we can handle. It happens. It's just a problem to be solved. I call this "temporary trouble." All we have to do is make the right decision; do the right thing; take care of business; and we can make the trouble go away.

But there's another type of trouble. We don't handle it; it handles us. All I know to call it is traumatic, terrible trouble. Sooner or later, we all get blind-sided by this traumatic, terrible trouble. It can start in different places—a fractured friendship; a spouse who doesn't love us anymore; a child addicted to drugs; a parent with Alzheimer's; cancer; foreclosure; losing someone we love. Traumatic, terrible trouble can start from any number of places, but it always ends in the same place—a hammered, hurting heart.

I've had my trouble this week, and you've had yours. I don't know what trouble may be lurking around the next corner, but I know this: **Jesus is my Helper, my Hope, and my Healer when my heart gets hammered by hurt!**

Let me ask you this. Have you ever loved someone dearly and profoundly, and they loved you back in the very same way? Before this person came into your life, you had never loved nor been loved quite like this. It was like you were connected to each other at the deepest levels. To you, there was nothing better than being with this person, talking to this person and sharing life with this person. Have you ever loved someone so much, you could not imagine life without them?

Then this very person hammers your heart with hurt. They say something deeply devastating. When you hear it, you don't know if you can breathe. You don't want to believe what they said. What they said, they did not say to be mean. In fact, they said what they said with respect and love. They had your best interests at heart. They were just being real. But it really hurt. What they said crushed you. It hammered your heart.

If you can relate with that on any level, then you understand fully what a group of men felt as they were doing dinner with Jesus. In fact, Jesus was the One who said the unthinkable words that set their hearts in a state of severe agitation. Jesus had said, "Before this night is over, one of you will betray Me; one of you will repeatedly deny you ever knew Me; all of you will desert me; and I will lay down My life and die for you."

When the words hammered their hearts, it was like they'd been kicked in the stomach. Jesus could see it on their faces, in their eyes—the shock, the utter disbelief, the fear. Some shook their heads. Some dropped their heads. Some tried to hide their tears.

Jesus waited a moment. When He had all of their attention, He said: *"Do not let your hearts be troubled!"* (John 14:1 NIV).

Where do you need to hear Jesus whisper or sigh or sing these words over your life? *"Do not let your heart be troubled!"*

DAY 31

When our little grandchildren are hurting or they don't feel good or they're just worn out, we rock them. We wrap our arms around them and sing to them. That's what Jesus longs to do with you when you're hurting or you're just worn out or your heart's been hammered. Jesus wants to take you in His arms, rock you, and sing to you, "Do not let your heart be troubled!"

Jesus uses a very unique Greek word here for "trouble." It means "an inner, agitating anxiety." Jesus is saying, "Don't let worry and fear shake your heart to pieces."

The word Jesus uses for "heart" is "kardia," like our word "cardiac." But it does not mean that major organ, pulsating in your chest. It means, "the center of all your thoughts and emotions."

Jesus is saying it's possible for traumatic, terrible trouble to be the reality on the outside. Yet, on the inside, there is no trouble; only peace and calm; an inner quiet unaffected by the crazy chaos on the outside.

You're probably thinking the same thing the dinner companions of Jesus were thinking: "How does that work?"

The Apostle Paul certainly knew how it worked. *"Do not be anxious about anything, but in every situation, by prayer and petition, with thanksgiving, present your requests to God. And the peace of God, which transcends all understanding, will guard your hearts and minds in Christ Jesus!"* (Philippians 4:7 NIV).

Paul goes on to tell us how to have a trouble-free, worry-free heart. *"Whatever is true; whatever is noble; whatever is right; whatever is pure; whatever is lovely; whatever is admirable—if anything is excellent or praiseworthy—think about such things...And the God of peace will be with you!"* (Philippians 4:8,9 NIV).

Notice that every possibility of experiencing the peace of Christ starts with your thinking. But this is significantly more than positive thinking for a positive emotional experience. First, we are promised the peace of God IN us, which passes all understanding. This promise is conditioned on our refusal to be shaken by trouble and our refocusing on all we have to be thankful for. Thankful thoughts set Jesus free to be our Helper, our Hope, our Healer.

But there's a greater promise than only the peace of God in us. We get God Himself—the God of peace—WITH us. Making the choice to keep our mind-set on what is true—the noble, right, pure, lovely, admirable, excellent, and praiseworthy— this makes us irresistible to the presence of God. Jesus comes to us as Helper, Hope and Healer and we are *"transformed by the renewing of our minds"* (Romans 12:2 NIV). When *"we have the mind of Christ"* (I Corinthians 2:16 NIV), we have the peace of Christ IN us and the God of peace WITH us!

Today's Crazy Big idea: When *"we have the mind of Christ,"* we have the peace of Christ IN us and the God of peace WITH us!

Today's Crazy Scripture: *"We take captive every thought to make it obedient to Christ!"* (II Corinthians 10:5 NIV).

Today's Crazy Prayer Starter: "Dear LORD, how grateful I am that You care about my every thought and emotion. Thank You for being my Helper, my Hope, and my Healer. Help me keep my thoughts set on all things excellent and praiseworthy. You are worthy of the best of my heart and mind. Thank You for Your peace. In Your name, Amen!"

"I AM" CRAZY

"I AM" CRAZY
DAY 32

The last song had been sung. The final worship service of the weekend was over. As people were filing out, one of my friends approached me for prayer. Her daughter was in deep trouble, which put this mom in terrible, traumatic trouble. She did not know where her daughter was. But she knew her child was struggling with a heroin addiction. This mom cried and cried as I held her. We wept, and we prayed. We called down the goodness and loving kindness of God on her daughter.

Notice all the right spiritual steps this mom took to bring into play help from Jesus, hope from Jesus, and possible healing from Jesus. First, she made weekend worship her priority, praising the beauty of Jesus through her pain. She humbled herself before the excellency of Jesus. She was willing to cry out in prayer to the all-surpassing Jesus.

After our "Amen" in His name, this troubled mom went her way, and I went mine. And the Good Shepherd went after one of His lost lambs. One hour after that time of prayer, this mom gets a call from her daughter. Her child wants to come home. It was as if Jesus was sighing over the whole situation, "Let not your hearts be troubled. I got this. I'm working everything together for the good."

It's an unshakeable truth: **Get a faith focus, and the God of peace will be with you!**

This mom told me the truth about her trouble, and then we went to God for a greater truth. The greater truth of Jesus always triumphs over the traumatic, terrible trouble.

This is what had happened at that stunned dinner table with Jesus and His disciples. Jesus had given His friends some hard, disturbing truth. Then He gave them a greater truth that triumphs over any trouble. Jesus says, "All this traumatic, terrible trouble does not have to affect your secure sense of inner peace, if you *"Trust in God! Trust also in Me!"* (John 14:1 NIV).

When traumatic, terrible trouble hammers your heart, don't become an emotional basket case. **Trip the "trust trigger," and triumph will happen in your heart!**

Do you know what trips the "trust trigger" and releases the peace of God for your life? Anchor your life to the promises of God. Here's how this can work for you.

First, believe that God is greater than your trouble! *"Ah, Sovereign LORD, You have made the heavens and the earth by Your great power and outstretched arm. Nothing is too hard for You!"* (Jeremiah 32:17 NIV). Ask God to stretch out His arm and dominate over the trouble you're in.

Next, believe that God is absolutely good. Remember the meaning of the word, "good," as it relates to God. It means you believe God is breath-taking in beauty, and He makes everything beautiful in its time. It means you believe God is utterly perfect, and He perfects even the most imperfect of situations. It means God is all-surpassingly great. *"We know that in all* *things God works for the good of those who love Him and are called according to His purposes!"* (Romans 8:28 NIV).

Thirdly, believe God is able! *"God is able to do immeasurably more than all we ask or imagine, according to His power that is at work within us!"* (Ephesians 3:20 NIV).

That's just three out of three thousand promises from God's Word, substantiating that God can be trusted. What about Jesus?

Here's the truth about Jesus. Everything that is true of God the Father is also true of God the Son. But with Jesus there is something more, which He promises to His friends and to us. *"Do not let your hearts be troubled. Trust in God! Trust also in Me. In My Father's house are many rooms; if it were not so I would have told you. I'm going to prepare a place for you. And if I go and prepare a place for you, I will come back and take you to be with Me where I am!"* (John 14:1-3 NIV).

Jesus is saying, "This is how you can trust Me. My Father has a house—an enormously expansive house with plenty of residences and room enough for you. I'm going to prepare a place for you."

When I talk about the Clark house, I'm talking about the place where my family lives. When Jesus promises to prepare you a place in His Father's house, He is making it unmistakably clear that you are a member of God's forever family. Jesus is preparing a place, divinely designed for you in God's heavenly home. It's the place where you get to do what you love best with those you love most all in the exciting presence of Jesus.

Now the key phrase here is that Jesus is *"going to prepare a place for you."* This brings up two questions. Where is Jesus going? How will He prepare for us?

This dinner table conversation with His friends happens on the night before Jesus is crucified. Jesus is going to the cross. He will prepare a place for us in the Father's forever family and in the Father's house by dying on the cross in our place for our sins. He will take upon Himself all the punishment we deserve for all our sin—all God's judgment, all God's anger, all God's condemnation will fall on Jesus and crush Him to death. He will sacrifice His perfect, sinless life to satisfy the holy justice of God in our behalf. He will bear our sin in His dying body. He will literally be made to be our sin that we might be made right with God with all our sins forgiven.

Maybe you say you want in God's family. Maybe you say, "How do I take advantage of what Jesus did on the cross to prepare my place in Heaven?" The Apostle Paul lays it out, as a lifelong process of trusting Jesus and telling others that He is your Lord.

"If you declare with your mouth, 'Jesus is Lord,' and believe in your heart that God raised Him from the dead, you will be saved. For it is with your heart that you believe and are justified, and it is with your mouth that you profess your faith and are saved" (Romans 10:9,10 NIV).

Today's Crazy Big Idea: Trip the "trust trigger," and triumph will happen in your heart.

Today's Crazy Big Scripture: *"In My Father's House are many rooms. If it were not so, I would have told you. I am going to prepare a place for you. And if I go and prepare a place for you, I will come back and take you to be with Me that you also may be where I am"* (John 14:2,3 NIV).

Today's Crazy Prayer Starter: Dear Jesus, please give me the boldness to let everyone in my life know that You are my Lord. I believe You died to pay for my sins. I believe God raised You from the dead. I surrender my life in Your saving name, Amen!"

"I AM" CRAZY

"I AM" CRAZY
DAY 33

Have you ever said, "I am forever grateful for the work Jesus did for me on the cross. I'm glad to have the hope of heaven. But what about the traumatic, terrible trouble I'm in right now? I need help. I need hope and healing right now. What about right now?"

I'm glad you asked that question because Jesus climaxes this difficult dinner table conversation with a phenomenal "I AM" declaration that He is a "right now" God. Before I tell you what Jesus said, let me tell you what Jesus did for the troubled mom with the addicted daughter. As of right now, her daughter has been drug-free for 84 days.

Our Jesus is breath-taking in beauty, and He makes everything beautiful in its time. He is excellent in perfection, and He perfects our most painful imperfections. Jesus is all-surpassing in greatness. Here's how He describes Himself as a "right now" God: *"I AM the Way and the Truth and the Life! No one comes to the Father except through Me!"* (John 14:6 NIV).

When you need "right now" help, **Jesus is the "right now" Way!** He is the way through trouble of any kind, no matter how traumatic and terrible. Here's His wisdom: *"Do not dwell* on the past. See, I am doing a new thing! Now it springs up! Do you not perceive it? I am making a way in the wilderness!" (Isaiah 43:18,19 NIV).

Whatever "wilderness" you're living through in your family, in your feelings, in your finances, never give up. Give it up to Jesus. He specializes in making a way, where there is no way. He made a way to save Noah's family from an unprecedented global disaster (Genesis 6-9).

Jesus made a way through the fire for three Jewish boys. In fact, He joined them in the fire and got them out of the fire. The hairs on their arms were not singed, and they did not even smell of smoke (Daniel 3).

Jesus made a way for Daniel out of a den of lions (Daniel 6). He made a way for Joseph —a way out of prison and a way to the most powerful position in the land (Genesis 41).

Jesus specializes in making a way where there is no way, typified by His triumphant work on the cross to make a way for us to get out of hell and into heaven. So we can confidently say, "Wherever, whenever, however we need help, Jesus is the Way." **But He's more. Jesus is the "right now" Truth!** When you have the truth of God's Word, you have hope. Here's the "right now" truth: *"I can do everything through Him who gives me strength!"* (Philippians 4:13 NIV).

Here's more "right now" truth: *"If God is for us, who can be against us? He who did not spare His own Son, but gave Him up for us all—how will He not also, along with Him, graciously give us all things!"* (Romans 8:31,32 NIV).

Here's even more "right now" truth. *"In all these things we are more than conquerors through Him who loved us. For I am convinced that neither death nor life, neither angels nor demons,*

DAY 33

neither the present nor the future, nor any powers, neither height nor depth, nor anything else in all creation, will be able to separate us from the love of God that is in Christ Jesus our Lord!" (Romans 8:37-39 NIV).

As long as you have the Truth, you have hope. But there's more. **Jesus is the "right now" Life!** Wherever you need healing, Jesus is your life. If it's emotional healing, *"He heals the brokenhearted!"* (Psalm 147:3 NIV).

If it is spiritual healing or physical healing you need, then worship Jesus, the great I AM. *"Praise the LORD, O my soul; all my inmost being, praise His holy name! Praise the LORD, O my soul, and forget not all His benefits—who forgives all your sins and heals all your diseases; who redeems your life from the pit and crowns you with love and compassion; who satisfies your desires with good things!"* (Psalm 103:1-5 NIV).

How is all this potential healing of every kind possible? *"He was pierced for our transgressions; He was crushed for our iniquities; the punishment that brought us peace was upon Him, and by His wounds we are healed!"* (Isaiah 53:5 NIV).

Often when you go to a funeral, it's not unusual to hear: *"In My Father's house are many rooms…I'm going there to prepare a place for you!"* as if the words of Jesus are about going to heaven some day. But our Lord is actually using the "right now" words of His day for people who are "right now" in love.

If a couple was engaged to be married in the day of Jesus, but they had not set a date for their wedding, the young woman might plead with her husband-to-be, "When can I be your wife? When can we live under the same roof? When can we be married?"

Do you know the traditional answer given by the young man to his bride-to-be? He'd say, "Let not your heart be troubled. Trust God. Trust also in me. In my father's house are many rooms. If it were not so, I would have told you. I am going there to prepare a place for you. I'll come back to take you with me to be where I am."

This is why I take people to the village of Korazin when we visit Israel. Still standing there is a first-century ruin of family homes. It's easy to see a central family home with extra rooms attached on each side. It was the responsibility of the groom-to-be to go home and prepare a room for himself and his bride. The groom-to-be was eagerly at work for his bride-to-be's good. It was a sacrificial labor of love to give her a place in the family. He was doing for her what she could never do for herself.

The Church is the Bride of Christ. When Jesus declares, *"I AM, the Way, the Truth and the Life. No one comes to the Father's House but by Me,"* He's using the language of love to assure us that He is right now at work for our good. His sacrificial work on the cross makes a way for us to be in the Father's forever family. When Jesus conquered death and hell, He did for us what we could never do for ourselves. He is our Life!

Today's Crazy Big Idea: Jesus is our "right now" helper. He always makes a way. The Truth of Jesus is our "right now" hope. As the Life, Jesus is our "right now" healer.

Today's Crazy Scripture: *"I AM, the Way and the Truth and the Life. No one comes to the Father except through Me!"* (John 14:6 NIV).

Today's Crazy Prayer Starter: "Dear Lord, thank You for Your labor of love on the cross in my behalf. You have secured me in the Father's forever family. You are always at work to my good. You are the Truth that gives me hope. I love You, Jesus. Amen."

"I AM" CRAZY

"I AM" CRAZY
DAY 34

Can you name three of the most joyous moments of your life? Was one your wedding day? In the pictures, everyone's smiling in the ceremony and at the reception. But then marriage is hard at best and hurtful at worst. Half of all marriages are so joyless, they end in divorce. The joy of a wedding day is not always sustainable.

Maybe you would say, "The birth of my child"; but probably not the birthing of said child.

The joy of birth is awesome, but then comes colic, sleepless nights, teething, more sleepless nights, the terrible two's. Before you know it, the cute baby is a TEENAGER!

Or maybe your joy-filled moment was a huge accomplishment—graduation, promotion, a major achievement in sports. But the satisfaction of a diploma, a raise, or a trophy is sadly short-lived. For more joy, there must be more huge accomplishments. But who can keep up that pace? Joy seems so momentary.

Joy is a big deal in the Bible, appearing over 200 times in the New International Version. In the Bible "joy" is "a delightful awareness of God's favor" (Strong's Concordance). Joy happens; not when we focus on something we do but when our focus is on what God is doing. It's not our efforts but God's involvement that results in our joy.

The Psalmist sings: *"We're depending on God. He is everything we need. What's more, our hearts brim with joy, since we trust in His holy Name. May Your unfailing love be with us, LORD, even as we put our hope in You"* (Psalm 33:20-22 MSG, NIV).

The word "rejoice" also appears over 200 times in Scripture. My personal definition of "rejoice" is "to make joy happen." God takes care of His responsibility in the area of joy. He targets us with His gracious favor. Our responsibility is to see what God is doing, celebrate what God is doing, and share what God is doing with others.

This is how Moses explained it to God's people: *"In the presence of the LORD, your God, you and your families…shall rejoice in everything you have put your hand to, because the LORD, your God, has blessed you"* (Deuteronomy 12:7 NIV).

So let's do a little gut check on joy. How are you doing in the joy department? Be honest with yourself. Is pure joy a rare experience in your life? Do you have an occasional experience of joy in your life when things happen right for you? Actually, that's not joy. That's happiness. We are happy when right things happen for us. We are not happy if things do not happen right. But there's a universe of difference between joy and happiness. Happiness depends on right happenings. Genuine joy has staying power. Genuine joy hangs in there even when the worst thing happens.

You say, "Really! How does that work?" I'm glad you asked. I read a study on joy in *Psychology Today* recently. According to this article, there are five essential elements that inject your life with joy. I call them "Joy Jumpers": 1)Loving; 2) Being Loved; 3) Serving; 4) Being generous; and 5) Feeling significant.

According to the article, these are factors necessary in forming a life consistently filled with joy. However, a long time before these "Joy Jumpers" were discovered by behavioral science—2,000 years before—they were practiced and preached by Jesus, the most joyful person to ever walk planet earth.

But here's the big difference. Jesus did more than inform us about these "joy jumpers"; He actually imparts them to us. Jesus infuses us with these "joy jumpers." He gets us jumping for joy.

This is another strong reminder of how good Jesus is. Remember that "good" ("kalos"), as it relates to Jesus, means He is breath-taking in beauty, and He makes everything beautiful in its time. The goodness of Jesus means an excellence of utter perfection. But Jesus is more than perfect. He perfects what is painfully imperfect in the lives of those who love Him. The goodness of Jesus means He is all-surpassing.

One of the areas where Jesus is all-surpassing is joy. But it's not just that He is all-surpassingly joyful. It's more that He wants to put His all surpassing joy in us.

Here's the promise of Jesus, regarding our experience of joy. *"These things I have spoken to you, that My joy may be in you and that your joy may be full"* (John 15:1 NIV).

I love the way the Living Bible handles the words of Jesus. *"I have told you this so that you will be filled with My joy. Yes, your cup of joy will overflow!"* (John 15:11 NIV).

Your life can overflow with joy even when things don't happen right. This is what I want for my life—an overflowing joy substantial enough to stand and stay strong even when life goes wrong. I want to be able to cry out with Nehemiah, *"The joy of the LORD is my strength!"* (Nehemiah 8:10 NIV).

I want to show you how Jesus modeled joy; how He tried to inject it into His followers; how He pursued joy in the face of the worst possible circumstances.

I want us to practice: *"Looking to Jesus, the Founder and Perfecter of our faith, who for the joy that was set before Him endured the cross, despising the shame and is seated at the right hand of God!"* (Hebrews 12:2 ESV).

This was the practice of Peter. He looked to Jesus as His example for experiencing joy even in the worst of situations. This is what he wrote, specifically with you in mind: *"Though you have not seen Him (Jesus), you love Him; and even though you do not see Him now, you believe in Him and are filled with an inexpressible and glorious joy, for you are receiving the end result of your faith, the salvation of your souls"* (I Peter 1:8 NIV).

What if we give ourselves the challenge to practice the joy of Jesus every day? Paul says it can be done. *"Rejoice in the Lord always. I will say it again: Rejoice!"* (Philippians 4:4 NIV).

In his brief, four chapter letter to the church in Philippi, Paul uses the word "joy" 16 times. He uses the name of Christ 50 times. Know Jesus; know joy. No Jesus; no joy.

DAY 34

Today's Crazy Big Idea: Know Jesus; know joy! No Jesus; no joy!

Today's Crazy Big Scripture: *"Let the light of Your face shine on us. Fill my heart with joy!"* (Psalm 4:7 NIV).

Today's Crazy Prayer Starter: "Dear Lord, help me grow in my dependence on You. You are everything I need and more. Let Your joy be the strength of my life. I know Your love is never-failing, so I put my hope and trust in You. For Your sake, Amen."

"I AM" CRAZY

"I AM" CRAZY

DAY 35

I'm a terrible shopper, particularly if it's for something important. Part of my problem is that I'm cheap. I don't want to spend a ton of money, but I also want what I want.

On this particular shopping excursion, I was in Bethlehem in the Holy Land. I wanted to bring home something meaningful and at the same time inexpensive. Our time in Israel had been so full of rich God moments. What could I buy to help re-live all of my spiritual experiences without breaking the bank? I wandered around this olive wood store in what felt like a shopping stupor. But something caught my eye. It was small enough to carry around in my pocket or to wear on a necklace chain. It wouldn't cost that much. But it would provide me with a way of remembering my priceless time in the Holy Land.

It was an olive wood Jerusalem cross. A Jerusalem cross is actually made up of five crosses, representing the five wounds of Jesus—two in His hands; two in His feet; and one where the spear pierced His side. I love to use my Jerusalem cross and the five sacrificial wounds of Jesus to burn in my memory the five basic behaviors that generate the genuine joy of Jesus—loving, being loved, serving, being generous, and feeling significant.

One of my favorite places in Israel I love to remember, using my Jerusalem cross, is the upper room where Jesus met with His closest friends for just a few hours on the eve of His death. I remember that the setting for this supper is a simple and plain room. In fact, no one even made arrangements for a servant to be at the door to wash the feet of each dinner guest as they entered the room from the dirty, dusty streets of Jerusalem.

Sadly, on this night, no one was thinking about anyone but themselves—no one but Jesus, that is. His disciples were arguing about which one of them was the greatest—no Jerusalem cross for them—not loving, not generous, not serving, not significant.

Instead of a cross, they should have received a cruddy plaque that said "self-consumed and insecure." Insecurity and self-absorption are the very opposites of loving, being loved, serving, being generous and feeling significant. In fact, we are not loving, serving, and generous; that's what makes us self-consumed and insecure.

Do you want to get free of your insecurities? Be loving, be generous, serve, make a difference for others.

This Jesus story opens with these words: *"Having loved His own who were in the world, Jesus now showed them the full extent of His love!"* (John 13:1 NIV).

Jesus gets up from the dinner table. Heated conversation stops in mid-sentence. He goes over to a corner of the room where there's a pitcher of water, a basin, and a towel.

Jesus takes off His robe. Now He's dressed like a servant, wearing only His under-garment. Now, Jesus looks exactly like a servant who would be hired to wash feet.

He calls His disciples to Him. Jesus goes to His knees. One by one, He washes their feet until He gets to Peter. Peter backs away from Jesus. "No way are You washing my feet." Jesus said, "If you don't let Me wash your feet, you cannot be part of what I'm doing here." Peter said, "Well, if that's the case, wash every part of me."

Jesus responds to Peter. *"'A person, who has had a bath, needs only to wash his feet; his whole body is clean. And you are clean, though not every one of you.' For He knew who was going to betray Him"* (John 13:10,11 NIV).

Two things I want to ask you to remember. The first is Jesus declaring that these men are clean. This is important. I want you to remember that. The second is that among them was Judas, the traitor, who Jesus refuses to describe as clean.

Jesus climaxes this poignant moment with His disciples with these words: *"I have set you an example that you should do as I have done for you …Now that you know these things, you will be blessed if you do them"* (John 13:15,17 NIV).

Jesus models love, generosity, and serving others to make a significant difference in their lives. We are blessed with joy as we practice these same behaviors.

Now Jesus has them in the right, humble spirit to have this last supper with Him. He would take bread and wine, bless it, and tell them to eat and drink in remembrance of Him. This is why every weekend in our worship experience as a church, we participate in this same supper. We eat a piece of bread, representing the broken body of Jesus. We drink a sip of grape juice, representing the shed blood of Jesus. We are mindful of how lovingly, generously Jesus served us on the cross to make a significant difference for us. This is the spirit that readies us for this "Jesus meal" every weekend—a devotion to love, serve, be generous, and make a significant difference in others' lives.

In I Corinthians 10, the Apostle Paul offers this insight on the Lord's Supper we practice each weekend in worship. *"The cup of blessing which we bless, is it not the communion of the blood of Christ? The bread which we break, is it not the communion of the body of Christ?"* (v. 16 MEV).

I like to translate that first part this way: *"The cup of joy which we enjoy, is it not communion of the blood of Christ?"* Each weekend, as we partake of the Lord's Supper, we are eating and drinking the joy of Jesus.

Consider the words of Jesus: *"Unless you eat the flesh of the Son of Man and drink His blood, you have no life (no joy) in you. Whoever eats My flesh and drinks My blood has eternal life (eternal joy) ...Whoever eats My flesh and drinks My blood remains in Me and I remain in them!"* (John 6:53,54,56 NIV, words in parenthesis are mine).

When I take the Lord's Supper, I meditate on my Jerusalem cross and the five wounds of Christ—His hands (loving and being loved), His feet (being generous and doing acts of service), and His side (my sense of significance through my relationship with Him)!

The sacrament reminds me of the source of my joy—partnering with Jesus in His life of joy!

Today's Crazy Big Idea: Jesus modeled for us the practices that produce genuine joy—love, generosity, and finding significance through sacrificial service to others.

Today's Crazy Scripture: *"I have set you an example that you should do as I have done for you ...Now that you know these things you will be blessed if you do them!"* (John 13:15,17 NIV).

Today's Crazy Prayer Starter: "Dear Lord, please forgive me of the times when I am too wrapped up in myself. I want to be wrapped up in You and the joy of being loving, being generous, and serving my way into significance. Thank You for your loving sacrifice on the cross. By Your wounds, I am healed! For Your sake, Amen."

"I AM" CRAZY

"I AM" CRAZY
DAY 36

Everyone loves a field trip, right? The best learning happens outside the classroom.

Today, we join the amazing teacher, Jesus, on a field trip with His followers. The late night supper is over. That lesson is done. Now it's time to take the night's learning to the street. Jesus leads His friends, minus Judas, out of the second story room, down a flight of stone steps, and along a narrow path that leads to the temple of God. Jesus abruptly stops His disciples in front of the gates to the temple over which is a big, beautiful bronze vine. To Israel, this is what the Great Seal of the U.S. is to us. The Great Seal of the U.S. is placed at the center of the highest office of the land. This big bronze vine is at the entrance of the temple to show how important Israel is to God.

Jesus takes a moment to stare up at this huge sculpture of a vine. His disciples follow His gaze. Jesus then takes a step closer to His men, so that now they look at Him as He announces, *"I AM THE True Vine and My Father is THE Gardener!"* (John 15:1 NIV).

This is Jesus once again declaring Himself to be God—as much God as God the Father is God, equal with God in every way. Jesus is the Son of the living God. This is the final time in John's account of His life and work that He makes an "I AM" declaration.

Jesus points at the bronze vine and says, "That's only a symbol. I AM God, the True Vine. I am the real deal. And My Father is the Gardener." In other words, Jesus is saying, "It is My Heavenly Father who has planted Me on this planet. I am His Vine."

The purpose of a grape vine is to produce abundant fruit for the enjoyment of the owner. The fruit of Jesus is love and being loved, serving and being generous, so as to make a significant impact in the lives of others.

These are the only behaviors that produce pure joy. Jesus practices these principles all the way to the cross, where he dies as an act of generous love. Then like a seed, He is buried in the ground. But on Easter morning, He bursts out of the ground and bears a huge harvest of eternal life for all those who believe. That's what Jesus, the Vine, does.

But what does God THE Gardener do? *"He cuts off every branch in Me that bears no fruit"* (John 15:2 NIV). The vine sends life-giving strength to every branch, so every branch can bear fruit. There are branches that take the life of the vine but do not produce life, like Judas. Judas looked like the other disciples. He had received from Jesus, like the other disciples. But Judas was all about himself. He wanted nothing to do with loving, serving, being generous, or making a significant impact in others' lives. He was cut off.

These cut-off, non-fruit bearing branches are not even good enough for the fireplace, so they are just burned like so much garbage. *"If anyone does not remain in Me, he is like a branch that is thrown away and withers, such branches are picked up, thrown into the fire and burned"* (John 15:6 NIV).

But God the Gardener does more. *"Every branch that does bear fruit He prunes, so that it will be even more fruitful!"* (John 15:2 NIV).

When you receive the life of Jesus and you productively bear the fruit of love, service, generosity, significantly impacting other lives, God does a supernatural pruning work in your life, making you even more loving, more generous with greater significance.

How does this happen? Look what Jesus says next: *"You are already clean, because of the Word I have spoke to you!"* (John 15:3 NIV).

Remember Judas was the one disciple who Jesus did not consider clean because the Word of Jesus had no effect on Him. It's as we believe and live the Word of Jesus that we are made clean.

A branch could be attached to the vine. It could be receiving the strength of life-giving sap and still bear no fruit if it was lying on the ground and all dirty. The good gardener would lift this vine out of the dirt and clean it off, so it could produce fruit, just as it was designed to do. That's exactly how God the Gardener uses His Word in your life as you believe and live it. The truth lifts you out of the dirt; cleanses you of all guilt and shame and brings out God's best version of you—loving, being loved, serving, being generous, in order to make a significant impact with your life on the lives of others.

Do you see that it's nothing we do that makes us clean—loving, generosity, or willing to serve our way into significance? This is only possible through a relationship with Jesus.

Do you know how long it takes a branch on a grape vine to bear fruit? Three years. Do you know how long these disciples had been doing life with Jesus? Three years. Through those three years on various occasions, Jesus had made a stunning "I AM" declaration about Himself, claiming to be God. Now with His death only hours away, He makes His final "I AM" declaration. *"Remain in Me and I will remain in you. No branch can bear fruit by itself, it must remain in the vine. Neither can you bear fruit unless you remain in Me. I AM THE Vine and you are the branches!"* (John 15:4,5 NIV).

Up to this point, maybe the most personal "I AM" claim of Jesus is that He is the good Shepherd, and we are His sheep. A shepherd is very close to His sheep. But a shepherd and sheep are not one and the same. The life of the shepherd does not flow in the veins of the sheep. But a vine and branch are one and the same. The life of the vine literally flows into the branch, becomes part of the branch, enables the branch to produce. *"If a man remains in Me and I remain in Him, he will bear much fruit; apart from Me you can do nothing!"* (John 15:5 NIV).

This field trip was meant to teach His followers and us an unforgettable lesson. Jesus alone is the source of all love, generosity, and significance. He is the source of all joy.

DAY 36

Today's Crazy Big Idea: Jesus alone is the source of all love, generosity, and significance. Jesus is the source of all joy.

Today's Crazy Scripture: *"Remain in Me and I will remain in you. No branch can bear fruit by itself. It must remain in the vine. Neither can you bear fruit unless you remain in Me. I AM the Vine and you are the branches"* (John 15:4,5 NIV).

Today's Crazy Prayer Starter: "Dear Jesus, You are my life. I am in You and You are in Me. Your love in me makes me feel loved and enables me to be loving. Your generosity in me makes me generous. Your heart for serving in me gives me a heart for service. My life is truly significant because of who I am in You. For Your sake, Amen."

"I AM" CRAZY

"I AM" CRAZY
DAY 37

What has been your most painful, broken relationship? How many broken promises did it take to break the relationship? Sorry to bring up bad memories. But here's where I'm going with this: Broken promises lead to broken relationships—the more painfully broken the promises, the more painful the break-up.

Trust is the solid foundation of any relationship—in a marriage; in a friendship; among neighbors and co-workers; between parents and children. Trust is cemented by promises made and kept. In the most important relationships, it is the most important promises that are made and kept. Relationships are made strong by the strength of the promises made and kept.

This is why the resurrection of Jesus is so significant to Christ-followers. **Since Jesus rose from the dead for us, all the promises of God are available to us!**

I don't know exactly how many thousands of promises God has in His Word for you and me. But I know this: *"No matter how many promises God has made, they are 'YES' in Christ!"* (II Corinthians 1:20 NIV).

God has thousands of promises in His Word. They are answered "yes" for those who have a real relationship with Jesus. Let me give you two quick examples.

Here's a promise regarding answered prayer: *"'Call to Me and I will answer you and tell you great and unsearchable things you do not know,' says the LORD!"* (Jeremiah 33:3 NIV). That's awesome!

Here's a promise God makes regarding your work: *"The desires of the diligent are fully satisfied!"* (Proverbs 13:4 NIV).

You say, "That's incredible. I want my prayers answered. I want my desires fully satisfied. How do I get in on this action? Who gets these promises made by the Lord?"

I'm glad you asked. Here's who gets to lay claim to the promises of God: *"Through faith and patience (you) inherit what has been promised!"* (Hebrews 6:12 NIV).

This is amazing. You don't have to work for the promises of God. You don't have to jump through any hoops. You inherit the promises of God. But you inherit God's promises through faith and patience. These words lose their punch in English. I have to share with you what the author was actually saying, when he wrote them in Greek.

The Greek word for "faith" is *"pistis,"* It means *"surrender to."* Understanding this changes everything about our relationship with Jesus. Consider these scriptures.

*"For God so loved the world that He gave His one and only Son, that whoever believes in **(surrenders to)** Him will not perish but have eternal life"* (John. 3:16 NIV).

So Bible belief is not mere intellectual agreement, like I believe George Washington was the first president of the United States. The Bible word for "believing faith" means totally sur-

DAY 37

rendering to the Jesus you believe in—surrendering all of your life to Him.

Here's another example: *"Yet to all who did receive Him, to those who believed in **(surrendered to)** His name, He gave the right to become the children of God!"* (John 1:12 NIV).

Read through the Bible. Every time you see the words "faith" or "believe," read it to say "surrender." This is a game-changer. In English, you can have faith in someone and not totally surrender to them; you can believe in something and not surrender to it. But in the Bible, you only actually have faith and believe as you totally surrender. To truly believe in Jesus is to truly surrender to Jesus and then receive the promises of God.

After His resurrection, Jesus made it clear that the first act of surrender once you decide to follow Him is to be baptized. In fact, this is one of the promises of God. *"Whoever believes **(surrenders)** and is baptized, will be saved; but whoever does not believe **(surrender)** will be condemned!"* (Mark 16:16 NIV).

But faith/surrender is only half of the equation. Hebrews 6:12 says: *"Through faith and PATIENCE (you) inherit what has been promised."*

The Greek word for "patience" is *"macrothumias,"* which means *"refusing to surrender to your circumstances!"*

This is a huge one-two spiritual knock-out punch that wins for us the promises of God. We totally surrender to Jesus, but we absolutely refuse to surrender to our circumstances. We refuse to surrender to our weaknesses. We refuse to surrender to our limitations. We refuse to surrender to any difficulty life throws against us.

Where in your life are you presently surrendering to your circumstances? You know you are surrendering to your circumstances when you feel negative emotions like fear, worry, anxiety, anger, or bitterness. You know you are surrendering to Jesus when you feel *"love, joy, peace, patience, kindness, goodness, faithfulness, gentleness, and self-control"* (Galatians 5:22 NIV).

What will it take for you to surrender your life to Jesus? With machine gun rapidity, He fires off a string of promises in John 14: *"Whoever believes (surrenders to) Me will do the works I have been doing, and they will do even greater things than these...I will do whatever you ask in My name* (notice the link between our surrender and Jesus doing what we ask) (*"In my Name"* means *"for My sake."* When we surrender to Jesus, we begin to act and pray for His sake.) *I will not leave you...I will come to you...The one who loves me will be loved by My Father and I too will love them and show Myself to them"* (v. 14:12,13,18,19,21). This is just the tip of a 200-Jesus-promise iceberg.

The trustworthy Jesus cements our relationship with Him by His promise-keeping!

DAY 37

Today's Crazy Big Idea: The trustworthy Jesus cements our relationship with Him by His promise-keeping.

Today's Crazy Scripture: *"No matter how many promises God has made, they are 'Yes' in Christ!"* (II Corinthians 1:20 NIV).

Today's Crazy Prayer Starter: "Dear Lord, I cannot get over how much You love me. Your Word is full of promises for me. Out of Your love You gave Your one and only Son to die on the cross to pay for my sins. When You raised Jesus from the dead, it was irrefutable evidence that all Your promises are true. Praise Your holy Name, Amen."

"I AM" CRAZY

"I AM" CRAZY
DAY 38

The deadest times of my life—when my marriage went dead; when my parenting went dead; when I was emotionally dead and spiritually dead—all happened as a direct result of surrendering to the pressure of my circumstances and refusing to surrender to the purposes of Jesus. The defining moment of my life came when I decided not to live that way a moment longer. If Jesus had a dream for my life, I wanted to live it to the full. So now I live, clinging to Ephesians 2:10: *"For we are God's workmanship, created in Christ Jesus to do good works, which God prepared in advance for us to do."*

I'm not saying that fully surrendering all aspects of one's life to Jesus is easy or ever gets any easier. But I decided I'd rather deal with the positive struggle of surrendering to Jesus than all the painful, negative struggles of caving in to my circumstances.

Most people never experience God's dream for their lives. I didn't want to be like most people. Most people cave in under the stress and strain of their circumstances. So most people live **"closed-in lives"**!

Have you ever felt like difficult circumstances were pressing in on you—job difficulties, financial difficulties, family difficulties, emotional difficulties, health difficulties, addiction difficulties? Does it ever feel like the difficult circumstances of your life have your back up against a wall? Worse, does it ever feel like you're cornered with no way out?

If we let ourselves be cornered long enough, our closed-in lives start to be **closed-off lives!** We start to feel closed-off from other people. Our relationships with family and friends start to go flimsy and fragile on us. Sometimes, we withdraw from others. Sometimes, they withdraw from us. Worse, we can start to feel closed off from God.

That's when we painfully decline into having **closed-out lives!** We find ourselves closed out from love, closed out from personal peace, closed out from hope, closed out from joy and sadly, closed out from experiencing the powerful promises of God.

I want to introduce you to two sisters who found themselves closed-in, closed-off, and closed-out because they had sadly surrendered to the cruel circumstances crushing their lives. Their beloved brother had died. They had watched their brother's body deteriorate as he struggled, suffering with an agonizing illness. They were there when all hope was gone. A final raspy breath rattled in his throat. Then he died. They wept and wept as they buried him in a stone-sealed tomb that very same day.

These two sisters and their brother happened to be dear friends of Jesus. Jesus had been in their home many times, ate at their table, taught them, and laughed with them. They all loved doing life together. There was no place Jesus enjoyed being more than at the home of Mary, Martha, and their brother, Lazarus. When Jesus showed up at their home this time, Lazarus had been dead four days.

DAY 38

Here's something interesting. In that day, Jewish people thought that after three days, it would be absolutely impossible for anyone to come back from the dead. Their spirit had flown. Jesus showed up on day four to make and deliver on a promise of God.

When Martha heard that Jesus had come, she went out to Him. Mary wouldn't go. Mary stayed surrendered to her unthinkable loss. She was closed-in, closed-off, and closed-out.

Here are the first words out of Martha's mouth when she went to Jesus: *"'Lord,' she said to Jesus, 'if You had been here my brother would not have died'"* (John 11:21 NIV).

Notice the closed-in limits she put on Jesus. She thought He had to be immediately present for healing to happen. She thought Jesus could handle the sickness, but four days dead was too much to expect of the Lord. However, she was about to meet a Jesus—a no-limits Jesus—who made an outrageous promise and delivered on that promise with supernatural power right then and there.

I don't know if Martha saw something flicker in the eyes of Jesus. But at that very moment, she reached down into her soul and pulled a flicker of faith. She took a huge risk and quickly spoke her faith out loud: *"But I know that even now God will give You whatever You ask!"* (John 11:24 NIV).

That spark of faith got a phenomenal promise from Jesus. *"Jesus said to her, 'I AM the Resurrection and the Life. He who believes in (surrenders to) Me will live, even though he dies; and whoever lives and believes in (surrenders to) Me will never die! Do you believe (surrender to) this?'"* (John 11:25,26 NIV).

Read those verses again. When Jesus introduces Himself as "I AM," it's a declaration that He is God, greater than life and death. The Resurrection and the Life is all about Jesus. That last question is all about you. *Do you believe (surrender to) this?* Do you surrender to Jesus? We all need a Savior who is bigger than our circumstances.

That's exactly what Martha got. Listen to how she surrendered to Jesus: *"'Yes, Lord,' she told Him, 'I believe (surrender). You are the Christ, the Son of God!'"* (John 11:27 NIV).

SPOILER ALERT! Martha is about to receive an amazing miracle from Jesus. He will raise her brother from the dead. No more closed-in, closed-off, closed-out living for her. Life is about to get **wide-open** for Martha. A flicker of faith wins the favor of God!

Martha's experience of spiritual breakthrough is recorded in God's Word for you. Have the challenging circumstances in your life got you closed-in, closed-off, and closed-out? Jesus is ready to take your life to wide-open—wide-open with hope, joy, and peace.

For you, like Martha, all it takes is a mustard seed-size (Matthew 17:20) flicker of faith. You don't have to stay stuck in your closed-in, closed-off, closed out life. You have a Lord who is greater than your circumstances. When you refuse to put a limit on who He is and what He can do, Jesus is ready to show you what He showed Martha. He is "I AM!"

Today's Crazy Big Idea: We all need a Savior who is bigger than our circumstances.

Today's Crazy Scripture: *"I AM the Resurrection and the Life. He, who believes in (surrenders to) Me, will live even though he dies; and whoever lives and believes in Me will never die. Do you believe this?"* (John 11:25,26 NIV).

Today's Crazy Prayer Starter: "Dear Lord, You are an amazing God, the Lord of life and death. I surrender my life to You. I want to live your dream for my life freely and fully. Thank You for being patient with me. Help my faith to grow. For your sake, Amen."

"I AM" CRAZY

"I AM" CRAZY

DAY 39

This is like "Sister Act Part II." In Part I, Martha came to Jesus. In Part II, it's her sister, Mary. In Part I, Martha's faith in Jesus frees her of being closed-in, closed-off, and closed-out by her hurtful circumstance. In Part II, it was Mary's turn.

But there is a recognizable difference between Part I and Part II. The distinction jumps out at this point. *"When Martha heard that Jesus was coming, she went out to meet Him, but Mary stayed at home!"* (John 11:20 NIV).

Have you ever stayed home on Jesus? Your anger or your doubt keeps you closed-in, closed-out, and closed-off. You know Jesus is approaching, but you go into avoidance-mode. You play the martyr. You throw a pity party for one. You wallow in your grief. Your self-absorption keeps you away from the comfort of a selfless, merciful Jesus.

The quickest way to get to healing and hope is to get to Jesus as quickly as possible. As soon as Martha gets word that Jesus is on His way, she takes the initiative and goes to Him. So she gets help first; she gets hope first; most importantly, she gets Jesus first. Closed up in her house of grief, all she had was gloom and doom. But once she is in the light of Jesus'

"I AM" CRAZY

presence, He ignites within her a flicker of faith. She cries out, *"Yes, Lord, I believe You are the Christ, the Son of God, who has come into the world."*

As soon as her confession of faith leaves her lips, Martha sees something shining in the eyes of Jesus. She thinks, "Oh my gosh, Jesus is about to show up and show off. I have to get Mary."

She gets Mary. She gets Mary away from all the other grievers. *"She called her sister, Mary, aside, 'The Teacher is here!'"* (John 11:28 NIV). I like this. Martha could refer to Jesus in any number of ways. But she calls Him Teacher. This is awesome.

Our tendency is to want Jesus to microwave us out of our mess. But Jesus wants to grow us out. The Teacher teaches us out of being closed-in, closed-off, and closed-out.

There's something else important here. Jesus was calling for Mary. In the same way right now, Jesus is calling for you. He can't stand the thought of anyone staying stuck in their struggle. What's beautiful is that when Jesus called, Mary came.

"Mary fell at Jesus' feet and said, 'Lord, if You had been here, my brother would not have died'" (John 11:32 NIV). She's still closed-in, closed-off, and closed-out.

How does Jesus break through to Mary? He does it the same way He wants to do it for you. He says, "Show Me your struggle." *"Where have you laid him?' Jesus asked. 'Come and see, Lord.' Jesus wept'"* (John 11:34,35 NIV).

The Greek word, used here for "wept," means a single tear was sliding down Jesus' cheek. What did that tear mean? Did that one tear of Jesus carry all of heaven's sorrow over people who surrender to their circumstances and settle for closed-in, closed-off, closed-out lives?

DAY 39

If that's you, step into the scene. Feel what happens: *"Jesus, once more deeply moved, came to the tomb. It was a cave with a stone laid across the entrance"* (John 11:38 NIV).

I hope it touches you at your core that you have a Jesus who is deeply moved by the crushing circumstances that come against your life. This is not a Jesus who stands by idly. When you surrender to Him, He moves into action.

Just like Jesus wants to speak into your crushing circumstances right now, He spoke back then: *"'Take away the stone,' Jesus said"* (John 11:39 NIV).

I wonder how many times people stop miracles from happening in their lives by not surrendering to Jesus. Instead, they surrender to their circumstances. God wants to deliver on a promise, but they get nothing with their closed-in, closed-off, closed-out thinking. That is almost what happened to Martha when she blurts out: *"'But Lord,' said Martha, the sister of the dead man, 'by this time there is a bad odor, for he has been there four days."* (John 11:39 NIV).

The good news? This is a second-chance Jesus, who wants to say to us today what He said to Martha then: *"Jesus said, 'Did I not tell you that if you believed (surrendered), you would see the glory of God?'"* (John 11:40 NIV).

Where do you need to see the glory of God in your life? "Did I not tell you that if you surrendered to Me, you would experience the glory of God? Surrender to Me in your marriage and see the glory of God in your marriage. Surrender to Me in your finances and see the glory of God in your finances. Surrender to Me with all your mind and all your heart, and see the glory of God in what you think and feel. Did I not tell you that if you surrendered to Me, you would see the glory of God?"

"I AM" CRAZY

Here's how it happened for Martha, Mary, and Lazarus. *"Jesus called out in a loud voice, 'Lazarus, come out!' The dead man came out, his hands and feet wrapped with strips of linen, and a cloth around his face. Jesus said to them, 'Take off the grave clothes and let him go'"* (John 11:43,44 NIV).

Lazarus was not the only one brought back to life. Everyone standing there who experienced the glory of God was freed of their closed-in, closed-off, closed-out thinking. They had been wearing grave clothes too, and they didn't even know it. But they got free by surrendering to Jesus and experiencing the glory of God.

They got wide-open lives—wide-open to the glory of God; wide-open up to all the promises of God; wide-open to God's hope, joy, peace, and love. A wide-open life is what you get when you surrender to Jesus. Take off the grave clothes of closed-in, closed-off, closed-out thinking. Walk out in the wide-open joyous victory of Jesus.

Today's Crazy Big Idea: The quickest way to get to healing and hope is to get to Jesus!

Today's Crazy Scripture: *"Did I not tell you that if you believed (surrendered), you would see the glory of God?"* (John 11:40 NIV).

Today's Crazy Prayer Starter: "Dear LORD, I want to see Your glory put on full display in my life. Again today, I surrender fully to You. Please forgive all the times I drift into being closed-in, closed-off and closed-out. Thank You for giving me abundant life and enabling me to live it wide-open. You are the Son of God. In Your name I pray, Amen."

"I AM" CRAZY

"I AM" CRAZY
DAY 40

Do you have a bucket list? What do you want to do while you still have a life to do it? Do you want to travel to some place exotic, learn a language, learn to play a musical instrument, skydive, bungee jump, meet some celebrity, fly first-class, or hike the Grand Canyon?

On my bucket list, the number one thing I want to do before I die is visit the island of Patmos. I don't want to go there for the classy resorts or the great Greek restaurants or sandy beaches. I'm not interested in what's happening there today. I'm all about a supernatural occurrence that took place there nearly 2,000 years ago.

Approximately 60 years after Jesus was crucified and raised from the dead, He made an unprecedented appearance on Patmos. Heaven literally came to earth.

At that time, Patmos was a small, desolate island, used as a Roman penal colony. Think something like Alcatraz but with no facilities or cell blocks. The prisoners lived in caves. Throw in hard manual labor. It was all designed to make for a punishing, miserable existence.

"I AM" CRAZY

So Jesus was doing a little prison ministry, visiting an inmate named John the Apostle. John was confined to this isle for the crime of being a Christian. The Empire could not stop him from talking about Jesus. So they put him on Patmos. This whole penal colony experience had to feel like hell on earth to John because he was pushing 80.

What does it take to get you discouraged about your faith in Jesus? Put yourself in John's sandals for a second. He'd been a follower of Jesus since he was a teenager. He had been standing right there and heard the promise of Jesus with his own ears: *"I will build My church and the gates of Hades will not overcome it!"* (Matthew 16:16 NIV).

Everything seemed possible when John was young. Jesus was doing miracles left and right; healing the sick, casting out demons, walking on water, and raising the dead. John was there at the foot of the cross when they cruelly killed Christ. John was one of the first to see Jesus, resurrected from the dead. John was there the day the church was born with the miraculous outpouring of the Holy Spirit and thousands being baptized.

But it had been 50 years since John had seen Jesus in the flesh. Even with all of the hurtful struggle when John was on Patmos, he was not angry with Jesus; He was adoring Jesus in worship. In response to John's faithful, passionate worship, Jesus came to him.

This is incredibly important to remember: **When our life is at its worst, our worship must be at its best to bring the presence and power of Jesus!**

Here's how it happened for John. *"It was Sunday and I was in the Spirit, worshipping. I heard a loud voice behind me, trum-*

DAY 40

pet-clear and piercing" (Revelation 1:10 MSG, LB). Notice the spiritual sequence. Through the worst life can do to him, John worshipped his way into God's presence. So Jesus came to John and spoke into John's life.

Here's how it happened for John: *"I turned around to see the Voice that was speaking to me"* (Revelation 1:12 NIV). I love this. When Jesus spoke like a trumpet of triumph, John turned toward Him. This is the secret to get through the worst life can throw at us—keep turning toward Jesus with more worship.

Check out how John never stopped worshipping. *"When I saw Him, I fell at His feet as though dead. Then He placed His right hand on me and said, 'Do not be afraid. I AM the First and the Last. I AM the Living One. I was dead, and now look, I AM alive forever and ever. And I hold the keys of death and Hades!'"* (Revelation 1:17,18 NIV).

Notice that when we never stop worshipping, Jesus starts to touch us. This happens to you in worship on the weekend. If you get goose bumps; or if you feel the hair on the back of your neck stand up; or if you start to cry; or if something unexplainable goes off inside you, I believe that's Jesus touching you. When you love to worship, He loves to make you aware of His closeness to you.

But there's more here. Jesus touched John with His right hand. The right hand of the Lord conveys His rescuing power. The psalmist captures it like this: *"Show me the wonders of Your great love, You who save by Your right hand those who take refuge in You from their enemies"* (Psalm 17:7 NIV).

But Jesus does more than touch. He whispers courage into our souls. His message to John and to us is: *"Do not be afraid!"* (Revelation 1:17 NIV).

Maybe you want to say, "Lord, if You only knew what's happened in my marriage. If you only knew what's going on with my kids. If you only knew my financial issues, my health issues, my emotional issues. How is it even possible not to be scared to death?"

Jesus has a response for you. It's the "I AM" declaration He makes to John: *"I AM the First and the Last."* Another way Jesus has of saying this is in Revelation 22:13, where He claims, *"I AM the Beginning and the End!"* This means Jesus can see the beginning from the end. He not only sees and knows what's happening in our lives. He sees it before it happens. He wants to prepare us for what's going to happen. He joins us while it happens. He gets us through whatever happens. He brings beauty out of whatever happens. He perfects the most imperfect happenings. He bestows His all-surpassing presence and power; His peace and joy; His hope and love in everything that happens. Jesus is a good God in every sense of the word.

But there's more that Jesus wants to reveal of Himself to John and to us when life gets as bad as it can get. *"I AM the Living One; I was dead, and look now, I AM alive forever and ever. And I hold the keys of death and Hades"* (Revelation 1:18 NIV).

Jesus has already been through the very worst life and humanity can inflict on anyone. *"For the joy set before Him, He endured the cross!"* (Hebrews 12:2 NIV). On the other side, beyond the hurt and hardship, there's a joy unspeakable. Jesus went to "death" and kicked the doors off the hinges. He stole the keys of Hell itself.

Jesus is unstoppable. Humanity's inhumane, torturous brutality could not stop Him. Death could not stop Him. The grave could not stop Him. Hell could not stop Him. Jesus wanted John to know what He wants you to know. Do not be afraid. **Your faith in (surrender to) the great "I AM" makes you unstoppable!**

Here's our reality. *"Who shall separate us from the love of Christ? Shall trouble or hardship or persecution or famine or nakedness or danger or sword?…No, in all these things we are more than conquerors through Him who loved us!"* (Romans 8:35,37 NIV).

I've changed my mind. Being some place Jesus has been is not on my bucket list anymore. Number one on my list is to worship the great "I AM," where I am right now.

• •

Today's Crazy Big Idea: Your surrender to the great "I AM" makes you unstoppable!

Today's Crazy Scripture: *"Do not be afraid. I AM the First and the Last. I AM the Living One; I was dead, and now look, I AM alive forever and ever! And I hold the keys of death and Hades"* (Revelation 1:17,18 NIV).

Today's Crazy Prayer Starter: "Dear LORD, I worship You with all my heart. Please show me the wonders of Your great love, You who save by Your right hand those who take refuge in You from their enemies. My greatest enemy is death. But by Your death on the cross for my sins and Your resurrection, You conquered the grave and Hell for me. Thank You and praise You. In the ever victorious name of Jesus, Amen!"

• •

· "I AM" CRAZY

WITH GRATITUDE

To my son, Joshua, who came alongside me in this project. His insights and hours of work helped me be a better writer and create a better book for our church family.

To my my daughter-in-law, Marissa, who used her technical abilities to help me keep everything organized.

To Scott Fulk, my favorite graphic artist, who applied his skill and creativity to help get this book completed and ready for readers.

To my friend, Daryl Saladar, a selfless servant of Jesus, who invested his time, energy, and editorial expertise to improve on my writing.

To Robin Benskin, our awesome office manager, whose English skills are way beyond mine. Her gracious willingness to find all my mistakes and correct them helped make this book better than I could on my own.